SEASONS IN
THE SUN

With kind regards
Ragna Dahl.
1986

🌹 Alpenrose Press

Library of Congress Catalog Card Number: 86-71400

ISBN: 0-9603624-4-4

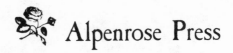 Alpenrose Press

Mail Order Department
Box 1888
Dillon, Colorado 80435
(303)468-2019

SEASONS IN THE SUN

By Ragna Dahl

with Mary Ellen Gilliland

TABLE OF CONTENTS

Acknowledgments

Our hearty thanks to all who contributed to *Seasons in the Sun*. A driving force that brought Ragna's dream of this book to reality came from her daughter, Freda Langell. Our special gratitude to Freda for her dedication, faith and sharing of experiences during this book's creation. Without the vital suggestions and material support of Hans Christian and Kirsten Hauge, *Seasons in the Sun* might have remained a dream. We appreciate Jack and Elsa Gilliland, copy editors, along with advisors Sheliah Mulvaney, Susan Locascio and Sheliah Gilliland. A rousing "thank you!" to Robin and Patty Theobald, whose generosity and patience in technical support earn lasting gratitude. For many long hours of manuscript preparation, typesetting and technical wizardry, we extend warmest thanks to "Mr. Computer," Larry Gilliland.

R. A. D.
M. E. G.

Chapter

A New King Comes

"Will the king wear his golden crown, *Far*? Will it be the same one we saw in the picture, with all the jewels on it?" I remember asking my father that question as I perched on his shoulders awaiting the arrival of a train bearing Norway's new king. "*Ja, ja*, Ragna, I hope so," Father chuckled. "After 500 years under a Danish, then a Swedish monarch, we Norwegians deserve to see our own new king in the ancient *Norsk* crown--and the royal robes as well."

I smiled. I was five years old and *Far* had chosen me from tamong my brothers and sisters to sit, tall as a Viking, on his shoulders today. *Mor* (that is what we called my mother) had carefully combed and braided my bright blond hair. I surveyed the crowd of family, neighbors, friends and townsfolk, dressed in the traditional red, black and white *Bunad*, the Norwegian costume. A radiant June day buoyed the high spirits of the 3,000 people of Steinkjer, Norway, as they milled about the railway depot, starched white aprons and embroidered red vests gleaming in the sun.

"Sivert Opdahl! *God dag!*" cried an excited young man. "Ah!" He clapped his hands. "We will tell our grandchildren of this day in 1906. A new railway, coming for the first time to Steinkjer, carrying a new *Norsk* king." He reached up to tweak my fat cheek. "And, you, little one, you will be first to see the small prince, Olav. You have the vantage point up there above the crowd."

Yes! Even if I were a gull soaring above I would have no better view, I thought. I watched school boys, my brother Jens' age, chasing

1

The Opdahl family home in Steinkjer, known for its "seven sisters," marked the town's edge where the forest began. House was bombed in 1940.

one another among shopkeeper's trousered legs. Shepherds had come down from the green goat pastures above. Sailors and fishermen had abandoned their nets and come from the blue fjord below. "Long live Haakon VII!" shouted some men grouped near the big wooden railway water tank. The musicians, with grandly carved and painted violins, began a lilting folksong. I liked to look at their rich black vests dancing with red, white and green embroidery. As they played, their white sleeves billowed in a salty summer breeze that also ruffled the Norwegian flag mounted proudly on a flagpole at the new railroad station.

"*Far*! The telegraph man said the train left Trondheim on time--7 a.m. sharp," my older brother, Jens, rushed up to say. "The king will be here soon."

My mother left the women to join *Far* when the muted sound of the train's shrill whistle floated over the noise of the crowd. Every-

2

one fell silent to listen and every eye turned to watch. Soon the huge black locomotive, shiny and new, steamed into sight. The locomotive made a great noise and scared the horses. As it grew closer, I clung to *Far*'s neck, for the new steam engine was huge and frightening. The monster breathed a big: "Hufta!" Then it emitted a terrible "Scree-eech!" and lurched to a stop. The smoke stack sprayed cinders across my white apron. I glimpsed the royal family arranged in a window of one of the five wagons attached behind, but the king was jolted into the queen as the train braked and they all nearly tumbled over. They quickly regained their pose. "There is the little prince!" I cried. Three-year old Olav smiled from his father's arms and waved a Norwegian flag. His father, tall, dark-haired King Haakon VII and Norway's new queen, the dainty English princess Maude, smiled and waved from their royal rail car now stationed on the platform. I leaned over to *Far*, surprised to see tears wetting his red-blond whiskers. Like my big brother, Kristoffer, and my uncles, *Far* rarely showed his feelings.

Steinkjer went wild with joy. Men shouted the King's motto "*Alt for Norge*," musicians strained to play above the clamor, singers performed, women wept, horses reared and dogs barked.

. . .

I understood the excitement because *Far* had gathered his children around the kitchen table and explained things the evening before. My family was one that aired and debated ideas. Our neighbors thought of us as an outspoken bunch, strongminded and opinionated. Though I yearned to skip away after supper and play the long sunlit evening away--even to stay up for the late night sunset--I stayed and listened to the big people's talk. My brothers and sisters lined the table. Kristoffer, the eldest, had already left home, but Anna, Ingeborg, Sophia, Jakob, Jens, myself and little Marie gathered to hear *Far*. I was five and one-half years old that June of 1906.

"Tomorrow Steinkjer will celebrate," *Far* began, "not only the coronation of our first king since the 1300s but our deliverance from war with Sweden, by the grace of God--and the demise of King Oscar! Now, you older children remember last year when the town swarmed with soldiers." I remembered the soldiers. They had swarmed from our small military base, which was an important asset to Steinkjer, our tiny fjord town north of Trondheim in central Norway's Trondelag region. I remembered my pride when the soldiers had asked *Far* to examine their big horses, draft horses that farmers had relinquished for the war effort. I stood in awe as *Far*, a coachmaster, opened their mouths to survey their teeth, then checked their knees. I watched tearful mothers and young wives in the village as they spoke *"Farvel"* to sons and husbands. My own brothers were still too young for war, but laughing blue-eyed blond young men in uniform joked in the streets. As mobilization progressed, the young men's faces became grim. *Farfar* (my father's father) said they were determined to win Norway's independence.

Far went on. Norwegians were outraged by Sweden's refusal to fly the *Norsk* flag at international diplomatic conferences. Norway's legislative body, the Storting, passed a law establishing an independent Norwegian consular office. Sweden's king, Oscar, vetoed the law in June, 1905. That made the *Storting* angry. Lawmakers declared that since Oscar failed to provide for Norway's welfare, he could no longer be called Norway's king. The two-nation union collapsed. Sweden refused to let Norway go. Troops mobilized and tension rose. But just before the Scandinavian neighbors declared war in October, 1905, the aging Oscar abdicated in an effort to avoid bloodshed.

One of my most vivid memories is the day when church bells rang in Steinkjer. I had run home to find Mother spinning wool. "*Mor*! *Mor*! Bells are ringing everywhere! What does it mean?" "It means there will be no war, Ragna," my mother smiled. "The war with Sweden is over before it began."

"Norway was free to select its own king," *Far* explained. "We chose Prince Carl of Denmark. But Carl insisted on a mandate from our people. Norway held a popular vote and Norwegians upheld Carl by a landslide vote. He telegraphed his acceptance and arrived in our capital, Christiania, a month before Christmas. His coronation took place at the ancient cathedral in Trondheim just last week and now he is touring his new realm."

"That's the whole story," Father declared. "*Ja*, we have reason to celebrate."

And celebrate Steinkjer did. Seeing my country's new king--and the little prince destined to succeed him one day--became my most vivid childhood memory.

. . .

Lilac fragrance floated on the warm breeze. Sunlight splintered on the table as *Mor* ladled out the *melke grot*, a special porridge, rich with sour cream and melting with cinnamon and sugar topping, a festive dish for Midsummer's Night. My stomach fluttered as I thought of the fine carriage waiting outside. Father had taken the carriage from his livery business for family use tonight, just as he had for a wedding earlier in the year. My little sister had put on her new cap tonight, sent to her by a relative in North America, where many family and friends had emigrated. Tonight there would be a huge bonfire on the seashore, reflecting its great light on the water. All the little boats would be decorated with birch leaves and lights, even their outhouses. Accordian music for dancing on the pier,

The year's most magic evening came on Midsummer's Night. Fjord waters reflected a myriad of lights from boats and bonfires. The year's longest day offered children a chance to dance on the dock, run a race, stay up late.

games and treats would add to the fun. I liked the spoon and egg balancing contest and the one-legged race. I could run fast as the boys and promised myself a win. The military would march and the long light evening would energize the crowd. Not even the little ones would get sleepy because sunshine drove away darkness and dreams. Finally, very late that night, the sun would dazzle the revelers with a light show over the fjord. "You can't help to look, it is so beautiful," I told Marie, my next-younger sister. While it is dark, all the shore fires will reflect on the fjord. And soon, the sun will rise again, just as pretty. There's never a happier night than Midsummer's Night. I feel warm way down inside me. It makes me sure winter could never, ever come again."

Behind our stout two-story house in Steinkjer rose a forested hillside. A sun-dappled trail disappeared into the wood and some little steps led to birchwood benches. Lovers would sneak out at night and meet there, I knew from listening to my older brothers and sisters teasing. Farther into the forest, big, luscious blueberries and cloudberries grew. One morning in late summer, I smelled the aroma of coffee wafting up the stairs early and *Far* shook my shoulder. "Ragna, come have your *kaffe og kaker*. Then you and I and Jens will go to the forest to gather berries."

Nowadays it seems strange, but we Opdahl children grew up on morning coffee with our breakfast cake. I had to gulp mine that morning, then hurry to have *Far* boost us onto benches in a two-wheeled wooden wagon. He flicked the reins over one of his own draft horses. Father knew the special places for berries. In good years, we returned with buckets full. Jens and I bounced on the hard bench as the road grew rough penetrating the deep forest.

We children picked the yellow cloudberries and popped as many into our mouths as into our buckets. The piercing raspberry-like sweetness proved hard to resist. *Mor*'s red goat milk cheese and rye bread tasted delicious for supper. Afterward I grew sleepy. I heard a high constant whine and batted at my ear. I did not want to wake up but I soon did for the sound came from a front line attacker in an army of militant mosquitoes. They began to land and bite quicker than I could slap. Jens and I swatted and scratched while *Far* built a smoky fire to drive off the cloud of insects. When most of the mosquitoes had departed, I whispered to Jens, who was older, already seven years. "Do you think there are bears in the woods?" "I think I heard one breathing," Jens replied. We both peered into the trees. "*Far*, will the bears try to get us?" Jens shivered. Father turned from the fire and grinned. "No, I will keep watch. Besides, bears and mosquitoes both hate smoke. See? I will even light my pipe! No, they won't come near." Jens and I felt safe in the warm circle of *Far*'s presence and drifted to sleep while he smoked his pipe by the murky fire.

During that summer, *Far* taught Jens and me to handle the big quarter horses he used in his work. *Far* operated a heavy load hauling service, kept four horses for livery use, traded horses, raced horses, trained and bred horses. I liked to help *Far*. When the town doctor rented a horse, I rode along to the farms where he made sick calls. I learned to slide off the big horse and run to open the farm gates. At day's end, the doctor dismounted at his home, then I led the livery horse back to the barn. For weddings, *Far* polished the special carriage and draped the interior in white sheets. It looked like a story book carriage belonging to a princess.

Sometimes Jens and I stuffed the horses' bells with grass to stifle the clang, then raced the animals in a wild gallop across the open meadows. It was all I could do to hold on but I would risk anything to keep up with my big brother. *Far* lifted an eyebrow and asked why his precious horses returned wet, but we said we did not know.

One evening, *Far* came into the house with bloody hands, his suit torn and muddy. A headstrong animal had kicked out the wagon seat and dragged *Far* on his stomach. He held on, fearing for his life. His hands were deeply cut by the reins. "My dear," said Mother gently as she cleaned his wounds, "could you not have let the reins go?" "No, Marta. Not in training that horse. I had to show that stallion who is boss. If I had let go, we could just shoot the animal, for it would be of no use or good." *Mor* sighed, but I felt proud of my father and decided that I, too, would have shown the horse who was boss.

"How did you stop, *Far*?" I asked. "The wagon caught between two trees, my dear. I had the strength to get up before the horse trampled me. *Ja, Gud ske lov.* God be praised."

I loved my papa!

· · ·

I had my own experience with *Far*'s horses. I led one of Father's biggest horses through Steinkjer's town square one pleasant autumn afternoon. Solid three-story row buildings lined the wide street, their lower levels a patchwork of awning-covered shops and businesses. Turrets and Gothic spires rose above the rooflines, a fascinating jumble to my curious eye. An ornate gazebo occupied the center of the spacious square. On May 17, Norwegian Independence Day, the square would become a sea of townsfolk--singers, dancers, musicians and joyous game-playing children. But today the square lay quiet.

I led the horse in the direction of a river that bisected Steinkjer and flowed into the fjord. Its bridge provided the townspeople's only way to cross from north side to south side. Our home lay in Steinkjer's south side, with a farm district just beyond.

As I crossed the sleepy square, the horse snorted and tossed his head, suddenly agitated. I held the reins hard as the huge animal rolled his eyes and jerked his head, almost throwing me off balance. I was determined to keep the reins. I heard a strange sound, almost like the great railway's iron horse engine, but quieter. The horse had sensed it first. Suddenly, a noisy, scary metal monster roared around a corner. An automobile, the first I had ever seen. The horse reared in terror, lifting me several feet off the ground. Then I came down with a bone-splitting thud and was yanked up again as the horse tried to bolt and drag me. "Stop! Stop!" I heard myself scream at the plunging, snorting animal. I held onto the reins.

Then I saw two big hands grab the bridle. Another man held the horse's head. The men from the automobile were helping me. They calmed the horse but I continued to tremble. Tears squeezed out of my eyes and I continued home, bruised and shaken. Near home, the horse ran for the stable and would have dragged me into his stall had Father not been in the yard. *Far* understood but I said nothing to *Mor* or my sisters. They would say "Little girls must stay home and learn to sew, and let the boys wrestle the horses."

I was not about to stay at home and let life pass me by.

Chapter

Happy Family

"Jens! Jens! Where are you going?" Jens bent over his skis, dripping a tallow candle on the bottom surface and smoothing the wax with a piece of cork. "I am going to ski to the lake to see if it is frozen," he replied. "Oh, I will come too," I said. I raced upstairs to change from my nightgown. The sluggish winter sun had not yet risen, but I tumbled into my woolen leggings, my boots and little full-skirted coat, knowing it would be light soon. The day was cold. November had come and last night's snow had blanketed the hillsides. We children knew that snow transformed our forest into a quiet, secret world of white magic. It waited for us to explore. Like my brothers and sisters, I had learned to ski as a young child, just three years old. We Opdahl children routinely squabbled over whose turn it was to use the skis. Usually I skied with one sister in front and one holding on in back, or just used a single ski. Alone I followed Jens wherever he led. If he flew off a steep drop, I sailed behind him.

Outside the house I grabbed a second pair of wooden skis, lashed them to my boots with bamboo strands and looked around for a pole. Jens had the only one, a long light bamboo stick used for braking and steering. "No matter," I muttered, and struck off behind him.

Jens kicked and glided along the trail with the ease of a Norwegian born to his skis. His rhythmic slide through the forest seemed smooth as a winged sea bird on the fjord. My shorter legs worked hard to keep up with him, but keep up I would. If I ran out of energy, I would go on determination, because where Jens went, I followed.

The green pine forest, stippled by white birch trunks, sparkled with diamond dust from the new fallen snow. Jens broke the trail in thick powder, climbing through trees. Animal tracks--rabbit, squirrel, deer--latticed the snow. The long uphill trek ended on a crest where the blue fjord and snow-quilted hillsides came into view. Jens squealed as he began the steep descent to the lake. He sailed down the narrow trail, missing the trees that crowded in, whizzing around tight corners. I began slowly, watching my skis slice through feathery snow, seeing the glistening spray billow away from my ski tips. Then I bent my knees and ankles sharply to steady myself and shot headlong through a blur of trees and meadows. No pole broke my speed but the snow itself braked me slightly, giving a feeling of floating. Soon I shot out onto the lake and landed in a heap.

Jens laughed. I laughed too, lying in the white fluff and staring at the ice blue sky, light as my little sister's pale blue eyes. "Tomorrow, we'll bring our skates," said Jens. "We'll clear the snow. Won't it be fun to skate again? I wonder if the fjord will freeze this year? Father says it will be a cold winter."

The salt water froze only during the very coldest times. Only once had Jens and I lashed on our skates with leather thongs and ventured out on the fjord to join the other children and grown-ups already spinning and gliding across the ice. A few disgruntled fishermen stood on the quay shaking their heads at the frozen fishing grounds. But we whirled in delight, despite bitter temperatures. We carried hot baked potatoes in our pockets to warm our fingers. Mother would have *middag*, the midday meal, ready at one o'clock, with sweet hot milk to warm the skaters. "*Ja*, it is cold, very cold, when the fjord freezes," she would say. This fall the potatoes had frozen before we Opdahls and our neighbors had taken them from the ground. But the turnips and carrots lay safely in storage. Blueberry and lingonberry preserves from summer's golden days shone like jewels in jars stored with the milk and cream in the cold cellar under the kitchen floor.

That afternoon, my mother served a fish pudding. My family ate fish every day of the week but Sunday. The teeming fjord yielded a bounty of salmon, cod, herring and other delicious fish that amply fed all of Steinkjer. *Far* went to the quay early to buy the fish, then *Mor* scraped, cleaned and dried it. *Mor* mixed the fish with salt and pepper, onion and potato flour blended with milk. When *Mor* made fish balls, I helped roll, then *Mor* fried them in butter over the wood-burning cookstove. I mashed the potatoes that went with.

The boys, energetic Jens and mild, calm Jakob, sloshed in before *middag* carrying the water for coffee, cooking and dishwashing. *Far* joked that the coffee always tasted better after Fru Skjordal washed her family's clothes in the pond, but now the temperature had grown too cold for outdoor laundry--and *Far's* jokes. The water in the boys' buckets never proved to be enough. They spilled half of it on the way home. After *middag*, they had to carry the used water out and then spills didn't matter.

When time for *kveldsmat* (supper) came, *Mor* ladled up heaping bowls of rye porridge, sweet with syrup and milk. She baked her bread from oat, rye, or barley flour and we children loved *smorbrod* (buttered bread) with syrup.

After *kveldsmat*, we Opdahls, all book lovers, read stories. But the evenings I liked best (and *Mor* liked least) occurred when *Far* took down his tiny accordian to play old-fashioned Norwegian dance music. Kristoffer, Ingeborg and Anna ran laughing for the guitar, mandolin and violin. We little sisters rolled up the rug. Soon the house rang with the lively music. We danced folk dances, the polka and waltz until the floor boards began to bounce. But *Mor* slipped out of the room. "*Mor* is very religious, you know, Ragna," Ingeborg explained. "She believes dancing is a sin." "*Jasaa*," I nodded. "*Mor* told me it's a sin to sew on Sunday, and to go to the cinema and to look too long in the mirror, for it will make me vain." Despite *Mor's* disapproval, the merry music rocked the house on many occasions and we children danced till we felt breathless.

To offset *Far's* leaning toward music, dance and aquavit with the menfolk, *Mor* stressed Sunday school attendance and prayer. When my four-year old sister fell ill with scarlet fever, I asked *Mor* to help me pray to God to make me sick, too, so I could go to the sick place and be with my little sister.

Mor spun some nice wool to weave fabric for a dress for me. I loved *Mor* for dyeing it red and not a sensible navy blue. Though the high wool collar scratched my neck, little girls were not to complain, so I said nothing. *Mor* also knitted woolen underwear and dark leggings to keep us girls warm. *Morfar* (mother's father) made us all wooden shoes, wonderful shoes that I could run all day in, for *Morfar* padded the instep so that it never rubbed on my foot.

Sometimes we sisters, all strong-minded, would fight, but *Mor* just went on spinning or ironing or making fish pudding. "As long as I don't see blood. . ." she sighed. One evening *Far* sent several of us sisters to bed for squabbling. When he heard us still fussing and pinching each other, easy when sisters sleep three in a bed, he took down his strap and mounted the stairs, his heavy boots clumping loudly with each step. "You be quiet!" he raged. We screamed, "No, *Far*, don't spank us!" and wriggled. Both smaller girls managed to roll under me before *Far* whacked us three sharp blows through the thick quilt. It didn't hurt much at all, I thought in surprise, but later that night I heard *Far* praying to God in his room, asking forgiveness for his anger.

Parental discipline ran at low ebb at Christmastime when the tree hung heavy with fancy homemade butter cookies. Next day, however, the tree looked conspicuously bare. "Who ate all the cookies?" *Mor* demanded, surveying the gaunt tree. No one seemed to know.

I wore my red dress on Christmas day when Father and Mother bundled us into big bearskin rugs for the sleigh ride to our grandparents home. The snow crunched under *Far*'s feet as he loaded the two sleighs with brown fur bundles, each with one of my delighted little sisters inside. *Far*'s eyelashes had frozen and the telegraph wires were "singing" in the cold. I felt so good, snug and warm. When Father set the horses to trot, with Kristoffer driving the sleigh behind, the little bells rang in rhythm with the horses' gait.

We children talked in excited voices that split the cold air. "Remember the time *Mor* fell out?" asked Sophia. "*Ja, ja,* I wasn't hurt a bit," laughed Mother. "I was so bundled up, I rolled off like a loaf of barley bread, but I didn't feel a thing." We laughed and continued a gay conversation until someone spied the grandparents' little red house. Though the windows wore their Christmas coating of thick ice, a small circle had melted where *Farmor* (father's mother) breathed as she peeked out to watch for her grandchildren. We poured into the house, calling "Merry Christmas!" and *Farmor* ladled out mugs of hot chocolate. My little sisters took turns rocking on *Farmor*'s special rocker. *Farfar* had made the hand-tooled leather side saddle his wife used on her wedding day ride to the church into a rocking chair.

Then *Farfar* brought out Christmas presents for each of us. Tall and distinguished looking, *Farfar* with his heavy crop of white hair made a thin but merry Yule elf. *Farfar*'s hands wielded a knife with deft skill. He made wonderful sculptured toys for the children. For me, he outdid himself. My gift was a little Norwegian hand sled, the *sparkstutting*, sanded and polished to a shine. "Oh, thank you, *Farfar*! May I try it right now?" My little sisters accompanied me and *Farfar* outside. He walked with us to a little hill nearby, his heavy reindeer leather boots squeaking on the frigid December snow. *Farfar* made

My Little Hand Sled

the boots himself and had carved a deep tread in the leather heel so the boots would not slip. He wore a heavy hat of rabbit fur and a brightly-colored scarf that *Farmor* knitted over his dark woolen coat. His tall, courtly appearance was underscored by his quiet manner, for *Farfar* spoke very little. He only scolded when he lost his pipe and finally gave that up when he quit smoking to avoid losing more pipes. When we asked a question, he replied, "You'd better ask *Farmor*." *Farmor* did the talking for the twosome and she became the boss over the years, but my grandparents lived happily together, making a happy home for us grandchildren to visit. I held the back of the sled while little Marie sat up front to ride. *Farfar* smiled, a smile just like Kristoffer's.

"We must go in now. It is time for Christmas *middag,*" *Farfar* finally said. I remembered that *Farmor* would cook ribsteak, a Christmas Day tradition and a treat for a family that lived on fish (except for meatballs on Sunday). I was hungry. Would today's dinner be as good as Christmas Eve's? I trudged back thinking about it. The rice porridge came first, boiled in milk and served with a large dollop of melting butter and cinammon on top. Then my older sisters changed the plates and carried in the potatoes and *lutefisk,* a gelatinous boiled fish that turned to jelly if *Mor* cooked it too long. Around every corner for the next two weeks, I would find yummy surprises, dainty rolled cookies, creamy Christmas puddings, breakfast cakes bright with dried fruit bits and Yule glog to drink.

Christmas lasted from Christmas Eve until the day after New Years Day, a merry round of parties, visits to friends and relatives and entertaining guests at home. My birthday fell on the fourth day of Christmas, but *Mor* planned no special celebration amid the ongoing round of festivities.

. . .

Far joked with his friends about Norway's two winters: "One is white, the other green." Green winter was not too far off, I knew, when February's bone-chilling 30 degree and 40 degree below zero temperatures gave way to March's icicles and April's dripping rooftops. Calving time came, and with it *Farfar*'s special treat. He always brought the yellow milk that the cow produces just after her calf is born. My mother used the milk to make a special custard, sweet, delicate and delicious. "We almost lost *Farfar*--and the milk!" Father told us children at *middag* one April day. *Farfar* had crossed a still-frozen lake on the way back from the farm. As he walked, he heard a loud, ominous "Cr-ack!" Suddenly, his boots broke through thin ice and the old man sank into the icy water. "But first things first! He saved the milk," laughed my father. He held the bucket above his head and was able to place it on the ice and slide it away from the thin spot. *Farfar* broke away the thin ice, worn to nothing by a stream flowing into the lake, and climbed out onto a surface that would hold him. "Poor *Farfar*, he must have been so cold," cried little Marie. "Yes, but he is fine now," *Far* said. "He will live to nearly 100 like his fathers before him--and me after him! The Opdahls are a strong and healthy family."

14

Chapter

The Farm

The ice on *Farfar*'s lake and Steinkjer's river fractured and winter flowed away into the fjord with the river's broken ice. Summer's sun seduced the trees to put forth their first new-green leaves. I was almost seven and one half years old. Just when my feet, freed from winter's heavy footgear, felt light as butterflies over green fields, *Mor* delivered the unhappy news.

"Ragna, you must go to help *Tante* Cecilia on her farm this summer. It is time you began to work a little. Now, don't look that way! You will have plenty to eat with *Tante* Cecilia--good food--and heaven knows food for twelve mouths has become scarce in this kitchen. Your father will take you across the fjord on Wednesday to meet your *Tante*. She will drive you up to the farm from there."

I was speechless. Leave *Mor*? Leave Theresa and Marie? Jens will have wonderful adventures--without me! I will miss my own bed. I thought of my two giggling sisters and my feather pillow. I will be afraid. *Tante* Cecilia spoke few words, a cheerless practical woman. She was not a soft one to hug like *Mor* but a big bony farm wife who never stopped work to cuddle a little girl or smile encouragement into her eyes.

My eyes welled with tears, but I said nothing. *Mor* brushed flour from her palms and cupped my cheeks to look at my face. "It's best for all of us, Ragna. It will be all right. You will like the farm."

I will not like the farm! I will hate the farm! I want to stay here! I raged inside. I ran outdoors, crossed the road at the top of "my" hill and ran into the forest to hide in a shadowy glen I knew there. I sobbed and cried, "I won't go, I won't!" I stayed a long time and when I emerged, exhausted by crying, I knew I would obey my mother and go to the farm.

· · ·

White sails gathered like a flock of settling gulls as my father and I approached the Steinkjer quay. Fishing boats, bringing in their catch to sell, crowded toward the docks. Piles of silver-scaled fish gleamed on the docks as fishermen in caps, turtlenecks and rubber boots tossed the fish to a man weighing each on a scales. Others stacked the weighed fish in crates, while a man at a stand scaled, cleaned and fileted fish for sale to villagers. Long lines of large fish hung in pairs from along a wooden rack, their tails tied together to hold them. Across the way, a row of salt-eaten buildings fronted on the quay. Fish dealers, a maritime hall, nautical supply store and others occupied the two-story white buildings. Each structure had twin rows of windows peering like the eyes of an old man who only watches the world around him. *Far*'s friend waved from his skiff and we stepped in, handing over my little rucksack. The fjord danced with color, the golden hue of wooden hulls, the blue water, the bright red of flags. But the ride went too quickly. Suddenly the shore appeared and *Tante* Cecilia, in her horse-drawn *stolkjarre* was saying, "Hop on up. No time to waste. There will be milking to be done as soon as we're back. Sit there, Ragna. *God dag*, Sivert."

I bumped and rumbled like an old carton of discarded milk cans as the road wound up through the hills above the fjord. The high peaks still displayed their mantle of snow, but a burst of green greeted the eye everywhere below. We passed several farms, collections of sod-roofed frame buildings each on its sturdy rock foundation--solid protection from the frozen earth's chill. Each little valley hosted a farm. Every arable acre blossomed forth little sprouts from the late spring planting of oats, barley, potatoes and turnips.

"Four Norwegian miles for the whole trip," *Far* had said on the boat. "Two across the fjord and two more to the farm. Of course, we measure miles differently from our friends across the North Sea. One Norwegian mile equals six miles the way the British measure." He kept up a running patter, but every once in a while his eyes looked sad.

The sea miles seemed short, maybe like English miles would be, I thought, but these land miles stretched long and hot and dusty. I wore many clothes--most of what I owned--for I had no travel case or trunk. The woolen clothes lay heavy on my small body.

Finally, the farm appeared and Uncle Ole with pretty Kristen waving beside him. The four big boys stayed in the potato field. Kristen would marry soon, *Mor* had said. I said *god dag* and asked Kristen if I could see her wedding dress. "Oh, it's not finished yet, but you will see it, oh yes, and the embroidered bed linens I am making too." I liked Kristen, because she was sweet like my own sisters. I wanted to stay to help her in the kitchen, but *Tante* Cecilia said, "*Kom*, it is time you learned to milk, Ragna. Tomorrow morning the cows will be your chore because I must begin the shearing."

I followed my aunt to the barn. I was afraid. I didn't think I could milk those big cows. The green slopes, supported here and there by rock walls, rose toward the high granite mountains. A stream, swollen with snowmelt from the upper peaks, cut through the green valley, running boisterous over the rocks. The rough-hewn farm buildings displayed weathered plank siding that gaped with empty knotholes. Steinkjer buildings had many more windows. Here, a few tiny windows peeked through the gray wood walls beneath a topknot of bright green, the sod roof.

The barn smelled friendly to me.

"We have eight milking cows, Ragna. Now! You must sit down here, like so, and take two of the teats, like so, and squeeze, like so! First one, and then the other. *Tante* Cecilia's practiced grip brought forth long squirts of creamy white milk that shot noisily into the bucket. "Now you try." I squeezed but nothing happened. "Ah! More. Now squeeze." A little dribble of milk ran across my hand. "More, more. You keep working. Change to the other two teats when this pair runs dry." *Tante* Cecilia got up and began filling feed buckets for the cows who ate grain while they were being milked. Then she started milking herself. "You will milk four cows and I will milk four cows. Then you shall have your supper."

My stomach was yelling "I'm hungry!" inside me and I licked some milk from my hand. I felt famished after the long day's journey. The milk came in little squirts and dabbles. My bucket would never be full, nor the cow empty, and I would never eat my supper. I wanted to go home. I looked up at the cow's face to find her looking annoyed with me. "Well, you mean old cow, I will milk you. Just wait. I began squeezing hard one teat after the other. I will. I will. I will. I will. The milk squirted in unison as I repeated the chant. Soon I began to sing, "I will! I will!" and the milk flowed into my pail. It took a long time, but finally my bucket stood full.

"I'm done. I'm all done, *Tante* Cecilia," I squealed, jumping up. As I did, the cow started, shot out a foot and kicked me. I fell backward, sat in the milk pail momentarily and then tumbled onto the floor in a big spreading puddle of spilled milk.

I felt shame flooding my face. "Ragna! What did you do? Look at this!" *Tante* Cecilia yanked me up. "Oh, well, a feast for the cat and her babies, too," *Tante* said and led me dripping into the farmhouse to a much-needed meal and then to bed.

My new bed looked pretty. I ran a hand over its handsome wool coverlet, called *Akle*, a rich blend of dark red, gold and royal blue. I climbed in. The bed seemed so empty--I had never before slept alone--and a heavy sheepskin blanket nearly suffocated me. I didn't think I was allowed to take it off, so I slept that way, after shedding some tears. I felt both afraid and homesick. I was afraid of the big boys, afraid I'd never be able to milk eight cows, afraid of the strange ways at table and around the farmhouse. I missed Jens and *Far*'s hearty laugh and the comfort of my mother. I went to sleep and dreamed I was at home, in my own bed.

Things were better the next morning. Kristen went with me to milk the cows. The animals loved Kristen, their milkmaid since childhood, and several lay a lumbering head on her fragile shoulder. Next, I helped with some late planting. I worked very hard, harder than ever before in my life. My skin stung from the sun and my fingernails were rimmed with black when I washed my hands under the pump before the midday meal. I placed my muddied wooden clogs in a neat line with the others under the porch and entered the farmhouse.

I stared at the table. White *franskbrod* and rusks, waffles, salted herring, lamb, potatoes, turnips, soup, a heaped crock of butter, smoked salmon, pilsner beer in a pitcher, goat cheese... "Is today a holiday?"

Uncle Ole laughed. "What? A holiday? No. No holiday. Why do you ask?"

"Oh! Because the table looks like Christmas, so much to eat. You are having guests, then?"

"Oh, no. This is *middag*. Everyone is hungry. So, we eat! *Kom*, Ragna, sit down."

I sat down and they all teased me. "Oh yes, a holiday. It's Norwegian National Potato Day," joked one of the boys. "We celebrate that you learned to milk a cow today," said another raising his glass. I tried to laugh, but my cheeks scalded red. When the time came to get up and say a grateful "*Takk for maten*", I felt an enormous relief.

The summer days wore on. I grew used to the teasing. When I lost a front tooth I really bore the brunt of my cousins' jokes. If I pretended to come after them, they teased, "Just try it. You hit like a butterfly and you don't have the teeth to bite us."

The summer nights grew longer. I lay awake listening to the muted roar of a distant waterfall, the shriek of a fox and a dog's territorial bark. Sometimes an owl hooted from deep in the lonely forest. Nearby, plaintive cowbells rang and sometimes Kristen's voice floated on the air singing. Kristen sang a happy song but it made me feel sad. I ached to go home. I had told Kristen that very day, "When you ride to Steinkjer on your bicycle, may I come? If you tie a rope to the seat, I will hold on and run behind." That caused *Tante* Cecilia to look at me sharply. She seemed kinder that day. But they all said no, that I could not run behind Kristen's bicycle. It was unfair. I wanted so to go home. Each night big tears wet my pillowcase. If mother were here, she would stroke my head and sing a little. I went to sleep humming *Mor's* song, pretending she had come.

In the morning, Kristen combed and braided my hair. The milking went better these days. After carrying the milk pails to the dairy house, I helped *Tante* Cecilia finish the shearing.

Tante Cecilia used big scissors like pruning shears to cut the sheep's wool. She knew each animal by name. "*Kom*, Langli," she said as her strong arms gathered one into her lap. She soothed the animal, talking softly as she sheared. The sheep lay there relaxed and I watched as *Tante* Cecilia flipped him like an oversized rag doll to cut his other side. She hummed and talked and sheared for an hour until the sheep was shorn, looking nude and bewildered as he stumbled away to the pasture.

I helped *Tante* Cecilia to wash the wool, submerging the rectangular pieces and squeezing them in a large wash pot. We changed the water till finally it stayed clean. We dried the wool in the sunshine and then hung it up to begin combing it. The wool started out crinkled and matted but *Tante* Cecilia's deft hands used the two sharp square-shaped combs to smooth and stretch the fibers, finally producing a roll of combed fleece about one inch thick. I often wound the bobbins for my mother's weaving and I knew that this thick soft roll would become fine wool thread for weaving after it emerged from the spindle. I liked the calm rhythm of the spinning wheel, the smooth feel of wool in my hands, and the look of the bobbin as it grew fat with thread around its middle.

When July came and the high meadows turned from white to green, *Tante* Cecilia said, "Ragna, tomorrow we go up to the mountains, to the goat hut, to pasture the animals there and make goat cheese. You will take your cows and learn to milk the goats, too!"

"How long will we stay, *Tante*? Where shall I sleep? Is it cold up there?"

"We stay till September. Bring your warm nightdress. And don't worry--the hay in the loft will make you a nice bed."

The goats ran and danced, nearly 40 of them, skipping across the green hillside, frolicksome as never before. They knew where they were going. I had to run to keep up when the herd broke for the gate. *Tante* Cecilia seemed happy too, and I felt free in the joy of God's creation--bright flowers nodding in green mountain meadows, fresh, crisp air, snow capped mountain peaks piercing a blue-blue sky and the dazzling fjord far below. The clean Norse air made the scene sharp, cut like a cameo, the colors bright as embroidery thread.

Our little troupe trekked far into the mountains. When we stopped to rest, *Tante* Cecilia brought out a bottle of milk and barley bread sandwiches, thick with goat cheese. We ate some delicious wild berries while the goats munched the sweet mountain grass.

Later we arrived at the *saeter*, a tiny sod-roofed goat hut in a grassy alpine meadow. A large woodstove for cooking dominated the little building and *Tante* Cecilia's big cheese kettle hung nearby. I cooled my feet in a crystal brook, watching the water run over speckled stones and broken branches. The breeze blew cool. Above lay patches of unmelted snow that looked fun for sliding.

"Milking time, Ragna!" called *Tante* Cecilia. She showed me how to catch the she-goats and hold them, calm them, and help to start their milk flowing. But I could not both hold the goat and milk it. I spent all my time running after this one, then that, spilling the meager contents of my pail.

Tante Cecilia said I must sit on the goat to hold it. She grasped the animal to steady it while I climbed onto its back. "I am holding on," she assured me. "You bend over now and milk. Tomorrow you will be able to climb up on the goats by yourself and milk too."

I milked until my fingers ached. That night I dreamed of goat milking. I awoke early to the gentle music of cowbells and the soft sounds of the flowing brook. The world seemed at peace, quiet, kindly. I hopped out of my crude bed and found *Tante* Cecilia already up, stirring a huge cauldron of goats' milk over a low fire. "See, it's beginning to turn red, Ragna. *Geit Ost!* Good red goat cheese, my first batch here. Give me my bag of dried rennet. In less than an hour, you'll see the curd form."

I drank my coffee and ate some *smorbrod*. When I peered into the cheese kettle, a watery liquid had collected on top of the cheese. "Whey," explained *Tante* Cecilia. Then my aunt cut the curd into many small blocks and began squeezing them, plunging her hands deep into the mixture. This released more whey. *Tante* Cecilia placed the curds back on the stove to cook again. Later, I watched as they were strained, then shaped and wrapped tight in cloth. *Tante* Cecilia said she would use a cheese press to make the *geit ost* firm and hard. When it had aged properly, the boys would sell the cheese in Steinkjer.

At milking time, I picked a meek-looking she-goat from the herd. "Now, little one, I am not going to hurt you. Just relax--there!--while I climb up on your back. Nice goat." I got myself onto the goat's back and took a moment to balance, for my feet did not reach to the ground. "There, now, nice little lady goat, its time to milk you."

I leaned over to take the teat and press gently upward on the udder, as I had learned to do. Suddenly, the goat gave a little hop into the air and began a mad dash around the meadow. "Aaiee!" I hung on for dear life. The goat jumped the brook, grazed an outbuilding, ran through the goat herd, all in a hectic blur. I bounced on the goat's back, braids flying. The goat raced stiff-legged and erratic, a zig here, a zag there. Then the animal stopped with a jerk and began to graze. I tumbled off, glad I had not been thrown onto the sharp rocks that dotted the mountain meadow. "Now, just how am I supposed to milk you if you act like that?" I scolded the animal, who looked calm and innocent now. "You can just burst for all I care!"

I learned to milk goats and I learned to love *Tante* Cecilia, who was brusque but kind, and I learned to fall asleep without crying, even though I felt sad. But the day Tante Cecilia told me I could go home to Steinkjer, the pent up tears burst forth. I sobbed and laughed, then ran to collect my things.

Wild Ride

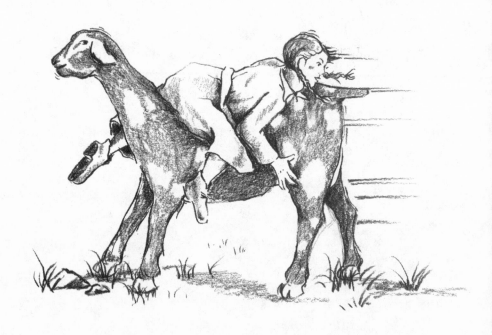

Chapter

The Dark

"Students, in the first grade, we will learn to read."

"Please, teacher, can we start right now?" I asked. I was anxious to read, to delve into the treasurehouse of books my brothers and sisters laughed and cried over. At age seven I said goodbye to my mother and walked with Jens and my sisters to this Steinkjer school. For the first time, I entered the big locked gate in the big iron fence. Latecomers must ring the bell to get in, I learned. The first grade classroom seemed large and important, with its line of inter-locked desks and its row of windows on one wall. Twenty boys and girls sat down in alphabetical arrangement by last name under the supervision of a pleasant-looking teacher.

I perched on the edge of my chair, awaiting the reading lesson with a mixture of eagerness and awe. Education was valued in my family. My brother, Kristoffer, the oldest, had gone to journalism school in Denmark, where he studied to become a writer. My sister, Anna, had also gone to senior high school (most continued only through the eighth grade) and studied English and German. She emigrated to California in North America where her language skills earned her a good job in a hotel. After Anna's education, *Far's* money ran out. Sophia and Ingeborg followed Anna to America. I spoke Ingeborg's name in hushed awe because she had won a beauty contest in California. She sent a newspaper clipping and *Mor* nearly fainted to see her own daughter's photograph in a public newspaper. Ingeborg wrote that she had become engaged to marry a gold miner.

"Anna and her sisters in North America! Imagine!" my grandmother declared. "All this schooling and reaching for the stars--even for young girls! In my day, we went to school for three weeks. I learned a bit of writing and some reading, then practiced on the Bible for many years." My older brothers and sisters laughed because *Mormor*'s Bible used the language of days long past--an ornate style, heavy with Danish words, a Norwegian language of medieval days. How she learned to read using that Bible and to write to be understood was a real feat in learning, *Far* said.

"School is important," *Mor* told us children. "I want you to earn an "A" in conduct, but first you must work for an "A" in achievement." We did work hard because the Steinkjer *folke skole* would provide all the education we could hope to get.

As autumn progressed, I left for school in the dark and came home at dusk. *Mor* kept *middag* in the cookstove warming oven for her school children. We hurried home very hungry after class.

One day, I had to serve the midday meal to my little sisters. Marie was no longer the youngest. Theresa had come three years behind her. The family had gone to a funeral and would be home soon. By the time I cleared away the dishes, the house had grown dark.

"Light the lamp, Ragna, I don't like the dark," said Marie. "But *Mor* didn't fix the lamp. It's empty. *Mor* said she and *Far* would come home soon after us. Just wait a little and they will be along."

"What's a funeral like, Ragna?" asked Theresa, looking big-eyed. "I wonder what it feels like to be dead."

"*Farmor* took me into her attic to see the family trunk where she keeps her corpse-cloth," I answered. "It's an old trunk, very pretty with rose painting all over it. Inside, she keeps *Far*'s baby clothes-- and even *Farfar*'s--and the cloth for her funeral. It is a fancy napkin with crocheted trim. She said it will cover her face and hands when she's laid out in her coffin. Then everyone comes to see you, when you're dead. They look at you in your coffin."

"You must look horrid, or they wouldn't have to cover your face," shuddered Marie.

"*Ja*, you do look horrid," I agreed. Actually, I had no idea how a corpse looked.

"Maybe you're already a skeleton and people can't stand to look at you," shrieked little Theresa. "Oh, I hope *Farmor* doesn't die and turn into an awful skeleton!"

"*Farmor* says they take your picture in your casket," I said reassuringly. "So maybe you aren't a skeleton yet, just very ugly. Anyway, they bury you quickly after they take your picture. Nobody

Ghosts and Skeletons

knows *what* happens to you down in your grave."

"Let's not talk about skeletons and graves!" Theresa shuddered. "It's too dark in here and I think I *heard* something!"

"What?" I was frightened too.

"I don't know. Something. A ghost I think."

"I'm scared! Where's *Mor*?" wailed Theresa.

"There are ghosts in here. Oh, no!" Marie began to cry.

My little sisters began to howl. I forgot about being the big sister and I cried too. I thought to open the regulator on the cookstove to get a little light from the low fire. But the girls saw shadows and netherworld creatures flitting about in the dim light.

Marie had the gasps by then, sobbing and drawing in her breath with little jerks.

Where are *Mor* and *Far*? I don't like the dark. How I wish they would come home! I cried inside.

I tried to comfort my sisters. I went to the window to watch for *Far*'s lantern dancing up the path from the barn. I went through the motions of being a big sister, but I felt very small and alone inside. Fear crept into my spirit on little spider legs.

When *Mor* came in, my sisters were close to hysteria. "I'm sorry, I'm so sorry we are late. The funeral went on and on. We could not leave the graveside before the others. Oh, I am so sorry. There, there." She comforted the little ones and calmed them with her presence.

I went upstairs to my bed. I piled the three pillows together, put my face into them, pulled the coverlet over my head and sobbed, "I hate funerals. I hate dead people. I hate the dark and I never want to be left alone again!"

Chapter

Breaking Rules

"Cr-rack!" Ole Thorsen's whip split the air over the rushing horses' heads. *Far* streaked forward, trailing Herr Blytt, the banker, who had a fine new thoroughbred. Steam from the horses evaporated into the frigid atmosphere. The river race neared its finish. I squinted from my perch on the bridge, straining to glimpse *Far* as he urged his horse ahead. Then *Far* gained on Herr Blytt. Jens and I were screaming, "Go. Go. Go!" Using the reins only, no whip, he cut close around a bend in the frozen river and eased ahead.

"He won, he won!" Jens cried.

We jumped off the edge of the bridge into a snowdrift and ran along the race course to join *Far*. We pretended to be horses ourselves, pressing to outdistance one another. The dry cold sucked all slipperiness from the snow covering the frozen river so our feet did not slip. My lungs hurt from the cold. Jens sprinted ahead and reached the finish first.

There was *Far*, head thrown back, laughing, straddling his sled in a sheepswool coat that hung to his knees to meet sturdy leather boots. He wore a big hat with ear warmers. The annual river race highlighted his winter. The men passed aquavit to toast him, calling *skaal* and "*ja, ja, skaal, da.*" They tossed off the aquavit and immediately downed some beer, wiping the foam from their moustaches before it froze. "It tastes like medicine," I whispered to Jens. "It's awful."

"I know. I tried some aquavit when *Far* left the bottle out." His eyes twinkled. "But beer tastes good."

Our boots crunched the snow as we walked down to the *torvet* near the Steinkjer pier. The marketplace, usually quiet on weekday afternoons, quickened on Sundays, though the *raadhus* where the town business took place and the *sparebank* where *Far* would deposit his race winnings remained closed. The postoffice and telephone office had drawn shades. A muted clacking emitted from the busy telegraph office. People strolled from the river race into the *torvet*, commenting on the cold, the gray fjord, the ice hanging from snow-frosted fishing boats. A dove-colored mist, like incandescent wool, rose from the fjord, veiling the scene in soft gray and blurring the sounds of conversation and footsteps. The fog made the bright red of a boat and the yellow of a fish box a surprise against the gray. This particular kind of mist came when the frigid air inhaled the warmth from the water.

Men stood in groups on street corners smoking. My Sunday school teacher passed, with a nod and smile. "*God dag*, Fru Janus," I called after her. I admired the young teacher's soft blue wool coat. When I am old enough, I will buy myself a coat like that, I decided. But I will never teach Sunday school. I could hear the teacher's singsong: "Jesus loves the little children," repeated with a bright smile. I didn't mind that. But the talk of hell-fire, the burning pit with smoke and brimstone, always made me squirm in my seat. It was scary to have to be good enough to avoid hell--like walking a tightrope over the burning lake that Fru Janus had described. Not that Lisa Janus didn't look nice or greet us children kindly, but behind her smile lay another face that took pleasure in frightening the class when she spoke of eternal punishment.

I was already a sinner. I had gone to the cinema once. Mother said it was a sin, a frivolity, though I didn't understand that because nobody laughed. Instead, the piano played soulfully and the audience dabbed at eyes brimming with tears when the heroine died in her fiance's arms. I came home with my brothers. My conscience pricked. Would I go to hell for visiting the cinema?

Noticing the gathering darkness, Jens and I scurried home, anxious to warm ourselves by *Mor's* cookstove. A wind blew from the fjord, its breath piercing our backs as we pounded across the bridge and down the hill toward home.

That night the pine trees whined in the brutal wind that came from the faraway North Sea. I imagined warring storm gods, angry as Vikings, hurling the wind like spears at Norway's huddled mountains. My sisters and I drew together under our quilt praying that a tree would not crash down on our home. "And God help those at sea," I prayed, repeating *Mor*'s favorite storm invocation. During the night, I awoke to listen to the lashing winds. Windows rattled and the house moaned. I lay wide-eyed in the dark.

The next morning, we children had to run to school in the stinging cold to avoid frostbite. "You must run all the way home, too," *Mor* cautioned. We had to run every day for many weeks, until the winter cold broke. When we arrived at school, a blazing fire waited. The teachers came early to make sure we could warm ourselves after our frigid trip.

The *folke skole*, Norway's free, government-run elementary school, taught me the 3R's, grammar, history, geography, natural science, religion, drawing, singing and Swedish gymnastics. Students attended five hours daily, with one holiday per month. Even the poorest child appeared at school scrubbed and clean.

Sometimes the gymnastics teacher took us out skiing, but on that first cold day school was all business.

"In 1888 Fridtjof Nansen skied across what unexplored northern country?" one of the school's three male teachers asked. "Greenland," a boy answered. "Correct." "What else did this famous Norwegian explorer do?" "He found a sea passage through the Arctic," another lanky blond boy volunteered. "And what happened?"

I strained my hand in the air. I knew. On July 21, 1893 Captain Otto Sverdrup sailed Nansen's ship, the Fram, from the New Siberian Islands. *Far* liked to talk about Nansen's adventures and I liked to listen. The Fram was lifted up and carried on the ice to open sea west of Svalbard. Nansen returned in August, 1898 to cheering throngs of Norwegians.

"His achievement was the most stirring event of the 1890s," the teacher went on. "Now, Ragna you look as if you are anxious to answer. Please come to the map and show us where Fridtjof Nansen crossed the Arctic."

My heart dropped. I could explain what Nansen did, but geography always undid me. I pointed an unsure finger at the Arctic Ocean, marked blue on the map. Somebody began to snicker. "They started at the New Siberian Islands," I mumbled, looking desperately to locate Siberia. "Ah, yes," the friendly teacher said, boosting my elbow. "You mean there." My hand pointed to the right place! "And what route did Nansen use to reach Svalbard?" He gave my hand another artful nudge. "Good. Svalbard, just above Norway. You may be seated, Ragna."

The bell rang. I bolted for the coatroom. I ran out to join the boys who attempted to pelt one another with snowballs. But the snowballs, dry as sugar, disintegrated. They settled for stuffing snow down one another's backs. Johan pointed at me, throwing snow. "Na, na, teacher's pet." I managed to trip him' but he jumped up and started teasing again. It was an old jibe this time: "Ragna is the circus lady, ha, ha, ha!" The other boys began to take up the chant. I flushed. The circus lady had come to Steinkjer last summer with a troupe that caused quite a stir--the first time a circus train had traveled as far north as Steinkjer. The lady had such big breasts that the clowns put a board across her chest and a man stood on it. I was just beginning to develop and I prayed to God I would never look like the circus lady.

"Ragna is going to get fatter and fatter till she can join the circus, na, na, na! I know how much you weigh. I saw the health chart," taunted Johan. I grabbed for him but he was little and quick. He jerked away. I chased and tackled him. He kicked me and rolled away. I scrambled after him, hot with anger. I caught his jacket. He lurched away.

"You won't catch me," he cried and ran toward the twin outhouses, squeaking into the boy's chamber just ahead of me. I pushed on the door. He drove it back. I pushed with all my strength. The door began to open.

"You can't come in here. You'll get in trouble," he screamed.

"I don't care. You're going to learn to shut your mouth!" I forced the door open and grabbed Johan, who kicked and yelled so loud the whole play yard stopped to watch. I dragged him out of the boys' outhouse, threw him face first into a snowbank, jumped on him and rubbed snow into his face until he pleaded for mercy.

"Are you going to stop calling me 'circus lady?'"

"No!"

"Then I'll never let you up." I shoved his face deeper into the snow.

"All right! I give up. But you'll be sorry for this," he choked, running off.

I slunk into the classroom, waiting for my gentle teacher to look at me with accusing eyes. I would be called shamefaced to the front of the class. Instead, he droned on about Roald Amundsen discovering the Northwest Passage in 1903. I could barely listen. I felt my classmates' stares burning on the back of my neck. "He deserved it," I hissed. A couple of girls turned to look at me.

"Amundsen now plans to journey to explore the South Pole, a dangerous and uncharted wasteland of ice," the teacher read. "He hopes to plant a Norwegian flag at the pole." His voice flowed on endlessly until the bell rang. I darted through the coatroom crowd and found Jens. "I'll walk home with you today."

We jogged through the streets together, skidding down the hills. I knew I could trust Jens to say nothing.

I went upstairs after school. My sisters were playing in the kitchen, so our room was quiet. Even if Johan deserved his lesson, I felt miserable. *Far* and *Mor* had instilled in me a deep respect for my teachers. I grew hot with shame at the thought that they might learn I had chased Johan into the boys' outhouse.

Last summer I had walked in the woods with some girl friends after a picnic. "I know where to find some raspberries," I called out to Anna and Kari, dancing ahead on the trail. There, just beyond a wooden fence grew big, luscious, red berries. "I'll get some for you." I reached my hand through the fence to let the ripe berries fall into my open palm. Suddenly, a man's gnarled, hairy hand grabbed mine. "What do you think you are doing?" a gruff voice demanded. My two friends skittered away.

My heart pumped with fear. "I just wanted a raspberry, sir," I stammered.

"What is your name?" the farmer asked.

I began to sob. Caught stealing! He would report me to the school. My teachers would know me as a thief!

His voice softened. "Well, run along--but no more stealing my raspberries."

"No! Never, never!" I cried.

I still felt guilty about the raspberries. Even when we Opdahls found a mitten lost on the ski trail, *Far* taught us not to keep it, but to hang it on a tree branch for the owner to retrieve. That, he said, was a Norwegian custom, for Norwegians were an honest people. I didn't feel badly about Johan. I would gladly teach him the same lesson again. I had no qualms about doing battle for myself or anyone who needed it, including several underdogs I regularly protected at school. But I could not bear to disappoint my kind teachers.

At 12 years old, I worked on my uncle's farm with Jens, age 14 (on my right). I contracted polio during an epidemic. But I refused to be sick. An amazed doctor later told my father, "Ragna's strong will healed her."

Chapter

Independence Celebration

"Books! New books," my brother Jakob cried as he came through the door, shaking bits of breath-ice from his muffler. He poured them out on the table. My eyes grew large. We Opdahl children hungered for books the way children in other countries yearned for chocolates. There glistening on the big kitchen table lay a collection of folk tales by Peter Christen Asbjornsen. I loved the old Norse stories, richly laden with witches, trolls and ogres, sly foxes and great bears, romantic princesses and country bumpkins turned heroes. The tales remained as alive as centuries ago, when the stories were first created and told during long evenings by family firesides. "*Brand*," Henrik Ibsen's great dramatic poem, lay next to *Amtmandens Dotre*, the women's rights novel by Camilla Collett.

My sister shot out a hand and snatched the folk tales. "I'll read it to you," she told Marie. Jakob wanted Collett's story about the Governor's daughters. I knew, because a girl he liked had just read it. So I picked up *Brand*. I had to wait until my kitchen chores were done to read it. Everyone in the village talked about Ibsen so I had heard about *Brand*. In the family, story people became as familiar as older brothers and sisters. My family could read aloud a book's first line and someone would guess the author. Around Steinkjer, conversation usually focused on books. "Marta Opdahl, have you read Alexander Keilland's new book?" the telephone operator would ask when *Mor* went to pay the bill. "No? Well, you must. It will make you laugh."

After dark, we Opdahls, like most Norwegian families, settled down to read. Stories opened a new world of excitement, fascinating characters and exotic places. When I was little, *Mor* used to open the regulator on the wood stove and read aloud by its firelight. But just when I learned to read, the family installed electric light. "What a blessing!" *Mor* exclaimed every time we turned it on. Then the family sat in the main room, where *Far*, who loved to be warm, fired up the heat stove to hellish degrees. *Mor* often returned to the kitchen to cool off. The single bulb on a cord from the ceiling illuminated the magic-filled pages of writers such as Bjornstjerne Bjornson, whose lively fairy tales delighted the children; Henrik Ibsen, the bewhiskered literary elf who wrote the famous *A Doll's House* and *Little Eyolf;* novels of the heart and home by Jonas Lie and the witty Alexander Kielland; Aasmund Vinje, a quaint and colorful poet of nature; Henrik Wergeland, the people's poet; and Knut Hamsun, eloquent advocate of Norway's soil and sea.

I devoured my new book. *Brand*, a poem Ibsen wrote almost a half century earlier, spoke to the deepest stirrings of my spirit. The priest, Brand, sacrificed everything to do what he considered right. He refused to hide behind excuses to avoid doing his duty. I loved him. Despite every kind of misfortune, he held on to his individual integrity. I found myself wanting to be a fighter like Brand.

I grew old enough to babysit after school and save a few *kroner* to buy books of my own. But mostly the earnings from child care and running errands went to buy clothes--a sweater perhaps, a pair of winter boots or black yarn for me to knit into the long itchy stockings that girls must wear, buttoned to garters to stay up. I learned to knit stockings with the other girls at school. We would knit or sew while the teacher read stories. Sometimes I used my small savings for Christmas gifts, hair pins for *Mor*, a handkerchief for *Far*--but often I went to my hiding place above the window sill and found my money gone. *Mor* had taken my little savings for some family need. "Oh, you shall get it back," my mother would tell me when I confronted her. "When?" I demanded. "I want it now!"

When summer arrived, Jens and I stuffed our few belongings into a pack and headed for one of the several farms belonging to our relatives. *Mor* wanted us to eat the good farm food--salted lamb and fish, butter and vegetables. We worked hard in return for our full stomachs. We planted oats, barley and parsnips. We cared for the children. We brought in the farm horses from the fields. We dug potatoes and turnips. Once I let the big butcher knife slip when harvesting potatoes and the sharp blade bit deeply into my hand. I held it up, streaming blood, to show Jens. We worked alone in the field, so Jens tore his shirt to bandage the wound.

Sometimes Jens tried his hand at milking. I loved being better than him at something. While he labored to get the milk into the pail, I pointed a full teat at him, called "Jens" and squirted him full in the face with milk. He looked so surprised. I laughed. He was helpless. For once, he had no idea how to fight back. I squirted milk into his hair and his face, even filled his shoes. Jens took cream from his pail and smeared it in my hair. We often returned to the farmhouse covered with dried milk.

. . .

When the manager from the cinema offered him a job running the film reels Jens no longer needed to work on the farm. *Mor* said, "No. It is a sin to work at the movie house," but Jens teased until she gave in. I vied for the opportunity to bring him lunch, an open faced goat cheese sandwich on barley bread with a bottle of milk. I stared fascinated at the film, but Jens was interested in his sandwich. While he ate he forgot to turn the reel. "Jens, keep winding!" I hissed. Then he cranked too fast. The audience buzzed angrily and the piano player rolled her eyes in disgust as she tried to keep pace with the slow down-hurry up film speed. I stayed till the end of the picture show, then emerged into the sunlight blinking, so enthralled I barely noticed the manager's frown as a small non-paying patron passed his ticket window.

Mor was waiting when I returned home.

"What took you so long? Did you watch the film? I told you to come right home!" she scolded. "Here, your father bought this little book from a missionary today. Read it and perhaps spiritual thoughts will cleanse your mind of the improper ideas those moving pictures introduce. Go ahead," she urged, pressing the book into my hand.

I needed no encouragement. A beautiful colored picture drew my attention: A lion together with a lamb, and a fair-haired boy child between them. "The New Earth" in fancy gold lettering appeared below. "The New Earth!" I read and breathed aloud. The booklet described a new world, sweet as Eden, promised by the Bible, according to the prophet Isaiah, chapter eleven.

"Look at this, *Mor*. It says our reward is 'the new earth,' not heaven. What does it mean?"

Mor, puzzled, could offer no answer.

I ran to find the Bible. I leafed through its parchment pages first in haste, then slowly--there was no book of Isaiah.

Mor sensed my frustration. "Maybe Isaiah is in the Old Testament, Ragna. We don't read that anymore, you know." She rummaged in a closet and finally pulled *Farmor*'s old Bible from a shelf. "Let's look," she said, blowing dust from its gilt-edged pages.

I could barely understand the book's lofty language, heavy with old-fashioned expressions. But I doggedly turned each page until I cried, "Here it is, *Mor*! Isaiah." Chapter eleven described a new world free of violence. "The leopard shall lie down with the kid," it promised. I read the booklet, hungry for details on this new earth God planned to create. I had never wanted to flit around heaven like a sappy angel anyway. I wanted to run and skip and ski, eat and drink, play with my brothers and sisters in the beautiful warm world God would recreate. The booklet denounced the idea of hell fire--I whistled in relief.

On Sunday morning I filed into the Sunday school room with the little book tucked snug under my arm. I had something that would turn that class around! As soon as the prayer ended, I raised my hand. The teacher took my book, smiling. As she scanned its pages, her sweet expession changed to a scowl.

"Where did you get this?" she demanded.

"My family got it, from a missionary man. He says the Bible promises a new world, with only peace and happiness. Isn't that wonderful, teacher? I want you to tell us more about it."

"Where in the Bible does the Scripture talk about this 'new world'?" she pressed.

"In the Old Testament. *Mor* looked in the closet and--."

"We don't use the Old Testament. That was just for the Jews!" Her voice took on a shrill edge. "Today we read the New Testament, the words of Jesus. Ragna," she said, leaning over to look full in my face, "if you do not believe that, you will not go to heaven." She stood up with a sharp nod. The case was closed.

"I don't want to go to heaven. I want to live on the new earth after I die."

"Oh, my God," the teacher gasped, looking around to check the children's querilous faces. "If you believe on this terrible thing, you will go straight to hell!"

"But the book says there is no hell. I'm glad, too. It says God is love and He would never torture anybody in hell fire."

The teacher glared. "Ragna, sit down. I will speak to your parents about this! Now class, please open your song books." She spit out the words. I sat down. When the class ended, each child carried his book to the teacher to get a gold star, pasted in the book for being present. I held out my book but the teacher stared past me. I got no star that Sunday.

My mother and father spent a tense hour with Fru Janus. I learned that *Far* had defended me. Nevertheless, I was no longer welcome in Sunday school.

The next week at recess time the school children avoided me. I tried to enter their games, but they refused to let me join in. "My parents told me I can't walk home with you anymore," my friend Sonja told me, looking at the ground. "I'm sorry."

Far said things would settle down. Indeed the resentment would have faded if two Oslo ladies hadn't come to town with a Bible entertainment called "Photodrama of Creation." They showed Old Testament stories in pictures on film slides. I begged to go. *Mor* said, "No!" I begged and teased. *Mor* said, "If it were in the church, maybe. But they're showing it in a worldly dancing hall. No daughter of mine. . ."

"Please, *Mor*. It's Bible stories. You want me to be religious. Surely, the Bible pictures won't hurt. And there will be no dancing during the slide show."

"Please, *Mor*."

"Please!"

"Please?"

"Well, all right. Go and get it out of your system!"

Mor lived to regret those words.

"A blasphemy!" a neighbor woman scolded. "Marta Opdahl, why would you let your own daughter go to see such a thing. It's a heresy. And Ragna showing rebellion at church makes matters worse."

"There's no sin in looking at God's creation," *Mor* answered the neighbors and all the other clacking tongues. "But she should have seen it in the church, *ja*, not a dancing place."

As for me, I imprinted the vivid images on my memory. Creation! Just the way the new earth would look! I gloated that I didn't have to go to Sunday school and squirm at the mention of hellfire. I knew the truth now. Let the two-faced Sunday school teacher worry about eternal torment--I was free of it forever.

Spring brought escape. I was glad to leave for Uncle's farm to work the warm earth planting potatoes. The lifted eyebrow, the cold stare, the playmate's turned back faded from my consciousness. But farm work proved exhausting. When I stood up too quickly in the potato field, I swooned. My spine ached. I had to force myself to

rise each morning. The mild May sun made me feverish. Jens
wanted me to be merry, but I could not.

May 17, Norway's national Independence Day, dawned. Uncle
shook my shoulder. "*Kom*, Ragna. If you and Jens want to go in to
Steinkjer today, you must get up and leave soon. I must be at my
chores before the day is gone."

Uncle had agreed to drive us half of the two Norwegian miles
from his farm south of town to Steinkjer. We would walk the remaining distance, and, if we wasted no time, be there for the one-
legged race, eggs-on-a-spoon contest, flag-raising, children's parade
and my performance on the harmonica with the school music class.
We bounced in Uncle's wagon. I felt sick. But I was determined not
to miss Independence Day. All Norway celebrated the anniversary
of May 17, 1814 when Norway had framed its Constitution and
gained independence from Danish rule. Children peddling their arti-
ficial mayflower would make the blossom prevalent as confetti
among the parade-goers. Though made of paper, the *mai blomst*
served as a proud symbol of Norsk freedom.

We waved good-bye to Uncle and Jens set a brisk pace on the
Steinkjer road. The rolling hills of Trondelag shimmered green in
the distance. A hundred little streams gurgled and splashed water
from snow melt on the high mountains, cutting a path to join rivers
and then the fjord. Waterfalls glistened on the cliffsides, their thunder muted by distance. Jens fairly danced along, his feet free of the
heavy.work boots. I walked in an increasing blur of pain. My back
ached, stiff and sore. Pain gripped my legs and every step became an
effort.

"Can't we rest, Jens? I don't feel good."

"We'll miss the parade. Look, we'll slow down if you like. Don't
worry, you'll feel better."

Finally we stopped under a tree. I lay back to rest. Up on a
branch perched a tiny cuckoo bird.

"A cuckoo, Jens! I'm going to make a wish." I kept my wish to
myself: I wished for protection from polio, a disease that had crip-
pled a number of my schoolmates. I felt a growing unease that I
might have caught this dreaded sickness. I cast the worry aside--it
was May 17 and we were already late. I got up.

When we reached the outskirts of Steinkjer, I walked wooden-
legged, every footfall jarring my spine in pain. Two nicely-dressed
ladies sat chattering beneath a birch tree. As Jens and I passed, their
voices fell to a whisper and I heard my name.

"What's wrong with you, Ragna?" one of them called.

I recognized the woman as a friend of my Sunday school teacher.

"She is sick," answered Jens. "Her back and legs hurt."

The two women exchanged a look.

"Polio!"

"No!" I insisted ignoring my misery. "Not polio."

"It is polio. This will be a punishment for you, Ragna, because you don't believe in hell."

"Oh! Is that where you are going?" *Mor* would have slapped me for that.

"No. I am saved by the blood of Jesus. But you--you will die and burn in hell!"

I felt something rising up in me. I refused to die. I refused to be sick. I refused to allow this hateful woman to triumph over me. I turned and walked away, Jens beside me. Slowly, heavily, I began to skip. I could feel the womens' eyes on my back. By sheer determination, I lifted my knees high and skipped away to the Independence Day parade.

Chapter

Growing Up

"Ragna! A package has come for you! From America!"

My sister Theresa's wooden shoes clattered on the pavement as she ran to meet me. "It's from Anna. Hurry and open it!"

I ran. Soon Confirmation, my rite of passage, would demand that I stop running, careening my sled through the crowds in town to scare the ladies, throwing snowballs at the boys and chasing after Jens. I would be a young lady. For now I remained free. I burst through the door into the kitchen. I liked to make a noisy entrance.

There on the table lay a box wrapped in brown paper, tied up with what looked like miles of string and stamped with the boldly colored American postage. I unwrapped the box with awe. I refused to rush with the first package I had ever received, though Jens, and my three younger sisters, Marie, Theresa and Solveig, the smallest now, all cried "Hurry! Let's see what it is."

Inside, wrapped like a butterfly in a cocoon of brown tissue, gleamed white leather shoes, low-heeled pumps with a fluffy cloth bow to tie over the arch.

"They're beautiful! White shoes! I'll be the only one at Confirmation with wonderful, wonderful, white shoes!" I began to dance around the kitchen, clutching the precious shoes to my bosom. "Oh, *Mor*, may I have white stockings, may I, may I please?"

Mor smiled. She didn't say no. I knew I would have the stockings, no matter what sacrifice *Mor* would make to buy them. I whirled about, singing, "White shoes, white shoes, white shoes" to the melody

41

of an Alleluia chorus the Confirmation class had learned to sing. I envisioned the white shoes shining like doves amid the serviceable browns and blacks at Confirmation. But the real reason for my joy was my anticipation of those beautiful shoes flying across the dance floor at Steinkjer's Centennial Ball, a festive party the whole town planned to attend. Wouldn't the other girls die with envy? The town would celebrate 100 years of independence and peace since Norway's 1814 Constitution and 100 years since Steinkjer's naming. Everyone had pitched in to build a new dance floor at my school. All the girls in my class planned to wear their white Confirmation dresses. "I'll dance like a fairy princess in these shoes!" I grabbed Jens and spun him around the kitchen, knocking *Mor*'s pots about in a boisterous polka until we sank laughing onto the wooden kitchen chairs.

Confirmation day came. In June, 1914, I posed in the photographer's studio, dressed in my white ankle length gown, with its covered buttons from neckline to hem and its lace-edged three-quarter length sleeve. I wore elbow length white gloves and a large white bow to draw back my long hair. I posed beside a fragile white desk, standing on a white fur rug. I couldn't have imagined a more elegant setting for my first formal photograph. I was really growing up.

My Confirmation portrait: Standing on the brink of womanhood, my hopes shattered with World War I's outbreak and my faithless fiance.

When the Bishop's voice rang through our only *kirke* (church), I was happy. No more weekly study sessions with those infantile boys showing us girls the dirty words in the Bible-- like "fornication" and "lust" and "unnatural acts." No more prating memorized answers. No more having to keep my mouth shut about my scandalous views on heaven and hell (*Mor* made me promise). No more being a little girl. And my first grown-up party to look forward to.

Not that I hadn't already tasted the spice of grown-up partying. Last summer, at age 13, I had noticed a poster advertising a dance at the labor hall. The artwork showed an elegant young woman and a handsome man waltzing. I determined to go to that dance. I eased out of the house and darted through a few house-yards until no one from home could possibly see me. Then I sauntered down to the pier, entered the hall submerged in a group of young people and stood alongside a pillar, watching the dancers. I picked out the best and followed their steps. The hall overflowed with young men, mostly soldiers in heavy boots, so all the girls were busy dancing. I was the youngest patron there. Self-conscious, I tried to melt into the pillar.

"May I have this dance, please?" a young soldier asked with a bow. I blushed to my belly. I couldn't believe he meant me. "*Ja, ja...* I mean, I think so," I stammered. The young soldier knew the Polonaise. The fast-paced polka broke all the barriers of strangeness. I turned flushed and laughing from the blond soldier to another requesting a dance. I danced and danced, until I felt a firm tap on the back of my shoulder.

"I believe this one is mine," a familiar voice asserted.

"*Far!*"

"Time to go home, my little butterfly. You're too young for this kind of thing. And you know *Mor* frowns on you girls dancing--especially with soldiers."

Far escorted me home, making it clear that my dancing days were over. But that was last year. Now, as a confirmed lady of fourteen, I had earned the privilege of attending the town party.

In August, just a few days before the Centennial Ball, *Far* rushed home at mid-morning with urgent news. War had erupted in Europe. *Far* said that Austria had declared war on Serbia for the assassination of Archduke Ferdinand, the heir to the throne of Austria-Hungary. Russia mobilized to protect Serbia from the Austrians and Germany declared war, first on Russia, then on the mobilizing French. By August 5, England had jumped into the fray to defend Belgium's neutrality against German troops marching through Belgian territory. *Far* predicted more nations would join the conflict.

My brothers and sisters clustered around *Far* and his newspaper. "What does it mean to us," asked Jens. "Will we have to fight too?"

"No, Jens. Norway is neutral. We will not fight. But we will feel the war's impact. People are already down at the bank demanding gold for their notes and buying up *kroner* for its silver content. The *torvet* is a madhouse. Everyone's stocking up on dried fish and tinned fruit by the cart load. So! You may have to tighten your belt."

"Why, *Far*, if there will be no war here?" Marie raised a puzzled face to her father.

"Because, Marie, Norway depends on overseas supplies. Many things, even little things like coat hangers and shoe polish, come from other countries. War can mean that commercial ships carrying these things, and more important supplies like coal and fuel oil, might not be able to reach us."

"Does Norway have any soldiers?" asked little Solveig, the last-born of my family's ten children.

"*Ja, ja,* the newspaper says our coastal fortresses will be ready quickly, in case there is a battle on the North Sea between the Germans and the English. King Haakon has called up nearly 200,000 Norwegian men to the fortresses at Christiania, Bergen, Kristiansand and even on our fjord at Trondheim."

"What else, *Far*?" asked Jens, excited about the mobilization.

"Just one thing." *Far* glanced at me. "The Steinkjer Centennial celebration has been cancelled."

"But not the Ball, *Far*. Surely, not the Ball?" I heard my voice go squeaky.

"The Ball, the children's parade, the picnic, the games... everything," *Far* replied, folding his large hands in resignation. "I'm sorry, children."

After a week of chaos, Norway settled down. Storekeepers' shelves had run bare and prices skyrocketed, but when no rationing order came, supplies gradually returned. The fjord was crisscrossed with steam launches, fishing smacks, tugboats and freighters as Norwegian mercantile vessels busied themselves hauling fish, wood, ores and nitrates to war-hungry countries. Except for the activity on the fjord, Steinkjer changed little. But for me, the war spoiled dreams of fun and romance. Until I met Reidar, that is.

Reidar! Even his name suggested manliness... romance... charm. "He is not what you would call good looking," I confided to my friend Kari the day after we met. "But he has a special charm. All the girls were falling for him."

I met him at a party given at the Forestry School in Steinkjer. Boys from all over Norway came there to study. Reidar's home was in Christiania, the capitol. His father was a doctor and his mother a piano teacher--an upper class status confirmed by the cultured Norwegian he spoke.

I had only to close my eyes to picture him again. His dark hair was nicely cut and groomed. His brown eyes were handsome, his best feature, I had already decided. I loved his courtly manners. All in all, Reidar was wonderful and I had fallen wildly in love.

I could scarcely believe that Reidar loved me too. He called me his *forloved* and gave me a gold ring. It meant we were promised to one another. I danced on my tiptoes to please him, trying to say and do the right thing. But my country dialect stood out like a rutabega nose, spoiling my gracious new image. I began to imitate Reidar's classic Norwegian, which sent Marie and Theresa into a chorus of giggles.

"Listen to her," they mimicked. "Allow me the pleasure of hauling your water bucket, my fair princess."

"And pray let me accompany you to the barn to scrub down the horses, my dear." They pranced around, imitating Reidar's genteel manners. I threw pillows at them till they quit.

In the springtime he told me of his transfer to another school. "You must visit me. It's only three hours away by train." He looked into my eyes. "I do hope you'll come."

I nodded. "I will. I will." Somehow! I whispered to myself.

Would *Mor* ever let me visit a young man in another town and ride all the way there on the train? I could ride for half fare during the student holiday. Perhaps *Far* was the one to ask?

When the big day arrived, I left for the station very early. The morning air stirred, cool and moist. *Far* drove me in the cart and helped to buy the round-trip ticket. *Mor* agreed on the trip only if I went and returned on the same day. I had brushed my hair until it shone against my shoulders, then smoothed it back to tie with a blue ribbon. I hoped the train dust wouldn't spoil my looks. I waved *farvel* to *Far* and cast about for a place to sit. The bench against the window felt hard when I sat down. I clutched the food basket *Mor* had given me and ran a hand over my hair. I remembered to act like a young lady. I sat up very straight and tried to look calm. But the screaming locomotive pulled the train so very fast--some said 15 miles per hour--and the cars careened around curves like they would surely disengage and fly off the track into the river they followed. I lurched in my seat and brushed black cinders from my skirt.

"Your first train ride too, *ja?*" inquired a fat, red-faced matron. "You are a little scared, I am sure." She bellowed over the train noise. I could feel myself blush. People began to turn their heads. "Well, don't be afraid, little miss. My husband rides this train every month. There's never been a summer wreck yet."

I cringed under the curious gaze of the surrounding passengers and turned to study the landscape. At mid-morning, the train pulled into a station and Reidar waved from the platform. We ate a nice meal together, barely noticing the food, then walked about the town. He took my hand when we stopped to sit on a park bench. I felt pierced with the sweetness of his presence. In a few years, when he finished school, we would marry.

"I must leave you, only for two hours. My weather science class. Please wait for me. Would you mind resting in my room while I am gone?"

I did not like being alone in Reidar's room. He had handed me a dull textbook, with pictures of trees and landscapes. Bored, I began to walk about his room, touching his things. I loved his beautiful clothes. I stood by the closet door, thinking of his wonderful blue wool jacket that felt scratchy against my cheek. I opened the closet and looked at all his clothes hanging there. Then I felt guilty and closed the door, a bit shocked at my own boldness.

He remained away for so long. I sat down for a while, then got up to examine a carved box on top of his dresser. Before I knew it, I had opened the top drawer and peeked in. Two sweaters and a familiar scarf. I looked in the next drawer, and the next. In the bottom drawer, I saw my own picture.

"What's this?" I gasped. Next to my Confirmation portrait lay photographs of three beautiful young girls. My heart sank. Tears flooded my eyes. Several letters sat in a stack beside the pictures. I tore them open. Love letters! Some of them my own, some from these other girls. My heart beat so rapidly I thought it would burst. I scanned the letters and threw them down in disgust. In a blur of tears, I wrenched the small gold band from my finger and placed it atop the dresser. I slammed the drawer shut and ran outside into the harsh sunlight. At the depot I buried my tear-streaked face in a ladies' magazine until a train arrived.

"Oh, *Mor*, I want to die," I sobbed into my mother's shoulder that night. "I am so disappointed. He said he loved me."

"There's a world full of nice young men out there, you'll see," *Mor* comforted. But I didn't want another young man. I wanted Reidar, the Reidar I first knew. My heart was broken.

At 15, I graduated from school. *Far* had no money to send me on to middle school, as he had been able to do for Kristoffer and Anna. In despair, I took a job as a maid. As I swept the floors, I remembered Reidar. As I boiled water for laundry, I swallowed the lump of his unfaithfulness. As I walked home from my work, I recalled our last bittersweet stroll together. *Mor* said that sometimes growing involved pain. When the river thawed at winter's end, *Mor* and I watched it wrench in violence. The cracking and breaking tore apart the ice. Yet the thunderous thaw birthed a serene river, flowing life.

Understanding didn't seem to soothe my grief.

"Ragna needs a change, Sivert." I heard *Mor*'s voice from below as I lay across my bed one evening. "Kristoffer has asked for someone to care for the children now while Bergliot is ill. Perhaps we should send Ragna to Christiania."

I perked up. Christiania! The Capitol! The ladies there wore fashionable clothes from Europe. My brother, Kristoffer, the author, mingled with writers and artists. Perhaps Kristoffer would help me to write a novel. Perhaps I would meet the King and Queen.

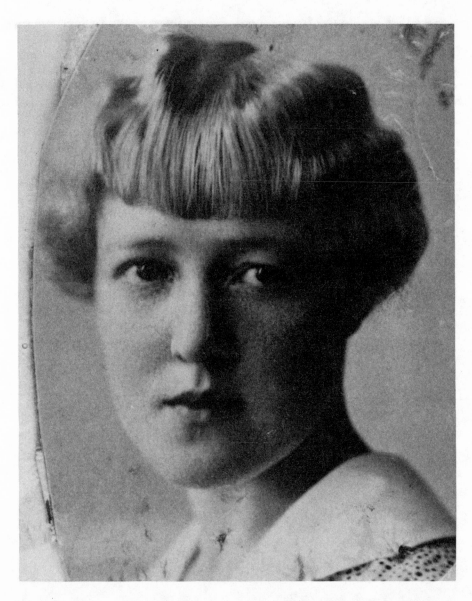

My 1919 passport showed an innocent face looking to an exciting future in London. Mor would have fainted to see I had "bobbed" my hair in Oslo.

Chapter

At Kristoffer's

My satchel sat on the luggage rack above as I perched on the railway seat, peering out the window at Trondheim, the ancient city of Norway's kings. *Far* had presented me with a booklet published by the railway company. It said Trondheim dates at least to Norway's first Christian king, Olaf Tryggvason, who established the city on its present site in 997. King Haakon had been crowned at the ancient Nidaros Cathedral here, just as St. Olaf had almost a thousand years earlier. The church's gothic facade displayed dozens of holy statues in ornate niches surrounding a huge rose window. I had never seen such a *kirke*. The little wooden church in Steinkjer seemed very humble in comparison. If I hoped to be a writer, I must notice everything and be ready to describe my travels. I made some notes in my book's flyleaf. The train moved on, leaving the old city to move into more rolling pastureland. Prehistoric rising and falling of sea levels had deposited a silt layer in this Trondelag region that made it Norway's richest farmland.

The train followed the River Gula through its fertile valley then crossed a bridge before a snack stop at Singsaas. Some passengers produced painted boxes or baskets filled with *smorbrod* and dried fish. Later, the train whistled into Roros, a tailings-littered mining town from Christian IV's time. The spired black and white church dated from 1780, I read. The booklet quoted a line I remembered from Ibsen's poem, *The Miner:* "Break me a way to the mountain's heart." I gazed at the mountains with new eyes.

The foaming Glomma River formed a waterfall near Berkal Sta-

Saying Goodbye at Steinkjer

tion. Accustomed to the rounded hills of home, I thrilled to a glimpse of the wild gorge of the Jutulhugget to the east. The Jutulhugget (The Giant's Blow) formed, legend says, when a mighty giant cleaved the mountain in one stroke to divert the Glomma's course into the Rendal valley.

"Norway's glory is her timber," the conductor informed me when I asked about the *lunns*, long rows of logs floating down the Glomma as it penetrated the huge Osterdal valley. Heavy forests climbed the valley slopes. Maybe Reidar would oversee this forest region one day, I thought. I already felt removed from Reidar. The sting had dulled.

At Koppang Station the passengers sat down in a large dining room for a 4 p.m. *middag*. They continued through a pastoral area to Rena and Elverum, at the end of the Osterdalen. Between there and Hamar, the train stopped at Loiten, a place where medieval pilgrims to St. Michael's Church offered prayers the same as in stories from England's Chaucer tales. At Hamar on beautiful Lake Mjosa the passengers had to gather their luggage and change trains, because the piecemeal-built railway switched there from narrow gauge to broad gauge track. I consulted my little book to learn that Hamar's cathedral collapsed under siege by invading Swedes in 1567 and peasants looted the building materials to construct farm out-buildings. I squinted at the structures nearby, trying to spot the ancient lumber.

Nowhere along the route did Norway's beauty outshine Eidsvoll, where Norwegians formed their Constitution in 1814 and declared their independence in an old timber-built manor house. My mind drifted lazily, remembering Independence Day at home. I dozed and awoke to find myself in what must be Christiania. The city stretched on forever. I caught sight of the island-dotted fjord, blue in the sunshine. The train slowed, then lurched to a stop at an old depot. An open square spread out before the station, a place where the city's tramway lines converged. I stared. I had never seen a tramway car. I shuddered to watch untended little children running behind one and jumping on while it moved. A grown-up man and a woman stood kissing goodbye in public. I stopped and stared. I had never seen such a thing. Foreigners, of course, I told myself. Norwegians would never embarrass themselves with a public display of affection. I scanned the crowd for Kristoffer. Who could find anyone in this throng? I had never seen so many people, men hailing porters, laborers unloading trunks, families standing in clusters awaiting the arrival of a loved one, sailors, soldiers, students and loafers.

"Kristoffer!" He stood out over the crowd, tall and lean, erect and aristocratic, the picture of *Farfar* with his distinguished nose and prominent forehead.

"Ah, Ragna. How kind of you to come to help us. How was your trip?"

I lapsed into excited chatter about mountains, waterfalls, cathedrals, rivers and historic cities, repeating facts from my booklet. I forgot that he had taken the same journey many times. "You wrote me that a writer must be observant," I smiled. "I decided to start with this trip. I've got more to tell you, too."

Kristoffer guided the carriage along Karl-Johan Boulevard, named, he explained, for Napoleon's general, Marshall Bernadotte, who became Norway's King, Karl Johan. The broad street sloped upward from the depot all the way to the Royal Palace. Kristoffer said we would drive by the palace itself. First we passed the *torvet*, the Market Square, where a statue of Christian IV, the city's 1624 founder, stood.

"Oh, Kristoffer. What is that beautiful tree?"

"An apple tree. I suppose you've never seen one. They grow only in the south. The apples are almost ready to be picked."

I drank in the beauty of the tree, hung heavy with delicious-looking red fruit. It looked like a painting, so perfect in its beauty. How I yearned to taste an apple... I turned as Kristoffer drove on and gazed at the tree. I had eaten apples only twice in my life, at a birthday party once and again at school graduation. I knew the sweet juiciness that burst in the mouth as one cracked through the red skin... In Christiania, maybe everyone ate apples. How wonderful to be away from Steinkjer and in a big city brimming with sights, sounds, tastes, smells!

Nearby, a *kirke*, the Church of Our Savior, rose. I saw the University with its Museums of Art and History, the romanesque Storting building, the Eidsvold-Plads and finally, the Royal Palace, a long, rather plain building set atop a hill in a pleasant park. "I thought it might be like a fairy castle," I confessed. I felt a bit embarrassed. I would have to begin acting more grown-up. Here in the capital, people displayed a sophistication unknown in Steinkjer. Girls my own age sat in the outdoor cafes wearing large hats and sipping coffee from delicate cups. I looked down at my brown traveling suit. It looked smart at home, but now the suit seemed plain and drab.

"Skjalg and Ingeborg will be asleep when we get home," Kristoffer said. "But you will meet your nephew and niece in the morning. They are looking forward to playing with you, *'Tante Ragna.'* They will be your charge until their mother is well again. I think you will like them."

. . .

I quickly won the children's hearts, for I was enough of a child still to want to play with them. When winter transformed the world to white, I taught six year old Skjalg to ski. We had wonderful times laughing at his spills. Three year old Ingeborg came along on the sled, bundled beyond recognition. At night when Kristoffer turned to his manuscript, I worked on my own novel, titled "My Proud Roots."

"I may as well get started now. I plan to be a writer, you know," I had informed Kristoffer.

"No. I didn't know."

"Yes, I will be a writer. I've already had an article published, in the newspaper at home."

"What? You?"

"That's just what the editor said. He even asked, 'Did you copy this?'"

"Well? What did you answer?"

"I said 'No!' I told him he had a nerve to ask. *Mor* says I'm outspoken and I'll pay for it. But the editor liked my story and he printed it."

"You may write your novel, Ragna, but I will not encourage you. Writing becomes a demanding mistress that dominates one's life. It's agonizing--and ambrosial. You'll need to spend your life caring for a husband and children."

"Why?"

"Why what?"

"Why are you so sure I'll be a *husmor*? I want to be a great writer, like Camilla Collett."

"You are a little rebel, *tulla mi.*"

"*Mor* calls me her little poet. We'll see who's right!"

. . .

Spring came early to Christiania in 1919. Sap stirred fresh green life in the trees. Strength flowed back into Bergliot. She began to take on more and more care of her children. I saw that the time had come to leave.

Kristoffer was working in his garden the morning I announced my plans. I walked down the stone steps to greet him. I loved my brother's garden, a lush little paradise. Kristoffer had a way with flowers. He grew raspberries and his vegetables tasted delicious, especially with the food shortages. Norway had imposed stricter rationing in January, 1918--a half pound bread flour per day and a half pound sugar per week. Worst was the limit on coffee, one-half pound per family per month. The rich bought butter on the black market, but working-class families were hard-pressed to keep their children's bellies full. I remember how we felt when the war ended. Armistice Day was November 11, 1918. All the restrictions on where we could go and what we could do ended. We looked forward to food being plentiful. I awaited the resumed flow of European fashions to dress shops where I spent pleasant hours window shopping. When I went home for Christmas, I learned of an organization that filled us with hope. My mother announced it one winter afternoon. I remember her reading the newspaper in the corner of a small sofa beneath a window she filled with geraniums. "Come, children! Listen to this," she called. "Leaders from all over the world have joined to form a League of Nations. Now countries will discuss their disagreements and work them out over a conference table. The newspaper says the World War was a war to end all wars."

Thoughts of ration and war lay behind us now. It was summer and Kristoffer planned to have an ample harvest from his beloved garden. He was thinning lettuce today.

"I'm going to London, Kristoffer. I have a position. It's all arranged."

He looked up, squinting into the sun.

"Bergliot spoke to her cousin in the employment office. The cousin found two Norwegian ladies in London who want a girl to cook and do housework. They're visiting Christiania now, but will go back to England in two weeks. I am going with them"

"But your passage...?"

"Miss Morrison said she and Miss Lange will lend me the money for my ticket. I will learn to speak English. I'm not disappointed about missing middle school anymore! Soon, I will be writing you letters in English!"

Kristoffer gave his blessing. He understood. I could not go back to Steinkjer, just as his lettuce could not retreat into the earth once it had seen the sun. A letter from *Far* cinched my decision: Uncle Martin had sent a ticket for me to come to North America. Since I was not at home, my brother Jakob had used my ticket and emigrated. There was nothing left for me. *Far* would object to my living in London. He would refuse permission. Kristoffer promised to write him, to explain. I felt new air under my wings.

On the evenings that Kristoffer did not work on his poems or his novel, he invited friends for conversation. I listened eagerly to talk of the Russian revolution, how the Bolsheviks had overturned the Czar. I hung on every word his author friends spoke, about the language reform that the Storting had passed, what the new division of language, establishing a language of literature and language of the people, would do to writers. They talked of the new prohibition law in Norway in 1919 and the effect of the 1915-16 worker reform laws. Labor was Kristoffer's pet subject since he championed the workingman in his books.

Bergliot, an author herself, joined in when conversation turned to language. Bergliot spoke a special dialect unique to Bergen. The language reform would affect wording of her book, the story of her childhood in the ancient port city. She had filled their home with paintings by artist friends and blended fine antiques among the solid Norwegian furniture. "She's not Norwegian!" Kristoffer's friends teased. "She's from Bergen."

I was drunk on these conversations, heady with my first taste of intellectual talk, mystified at first because I understood so little. But now I lost my appetite for Christiania talk. England beckoned. A new life! I knew so little--England conjured up two images: The Tower of London and Jack the Ripper. Nevertheless I woke up at dawn every morning alive with excitement.

I wanted to talk with Kristoffer the night before we sailed. I had a question to ask him. After I read the children a bedtime story, I found him smoking in the small salon and blurted it out.

"Kristoffer, do you believe in God?"

The whole family suspected he had become an atheist. He never went to church, not even on Christmas day.

He smiled. Kristoffer looked handsome when he smiled.

"Do I believe in God. . .? A good question, Ragna. Let me see. . . When I look at nature with its amazing variety, the four seasons, the myriad of animal life, I find I must believe that someone created it all. So. . . yes, I believe there is a God."

I had my second question ready. "Do you believe in burning hell?"

"Absolutely not."

"Why not?"

"Well, Ragna, the Bible, in the first book, Genesis, describes God showing Adam and Eve the forbidden tree. He said, 'If you eat of it, you shall surely die.' He did not tell the first couple on earth that he had a burning hell ready for them. The wages of sin is death--not hell, in my opinion."

I felt a weight lift from my mind. "Then why does everyone at home talk all the time about hellfire?"

"Oh," chuckled Kristoffer. "They have to have that doctrine, to scare people into being good."

I laughed along with him. Here was a member of my family with an open mind, someone who could see the truth despite what the *prest* forced down our throats. Kristoffer agreed with me! I didn't want to leave Norway a religious outcast. Even at 19 years, I had little desire to stand my ground alone quite yet. I suddenly felt very fond of my mysterious older brother. I smiled and left him to his pipe.

Chapter

London

I could feel little dots of perspiration on my forehead. Fishballs spattered in butter on the stove. Steam rose in big clouds from the potato pot. The table setting lay half done and the dinner too done. I was expected to answer the door when the guests came and my last white apron bore spots and stains from cooking.

Mrs. Morrison's sister arrived, ushered in by her chauffeur.

"Good day, madam," I said in English as I grasped her fur to my spotted bosom. As soon as she disappeared, I threw the coat on a chair and raced back to the kitchen. The sago pudding had set up. Mrs. Morrison had carried the bilberry juice to flavor the delicate dessert on the boat, then the train from Norway. The Norwegian dinner for her, Miss Lange and their guests celebrated a happy trip.

"You must speak English today, no Norwegian," Mrs. Morrison instructed. "And remember, it is *Mr.* Sheffield and *Mrs.* Jones."

I had already made the mistake of calling Miss Lange by her first name. In my job as a servant girl in Steinkjer, I called the master "Johan" and the mistress "Anna". I sat at table with them for *middag*. When I tried to sit down with my mistresses here, the horrified gasp was heard as far away as Balford Lane.

I brushed the damp hair away from my temple. Time to clear away the soup bowls and serve the fish. I smoothed my black maid's uniform and adjusted my white cap. I still hated wearing them. Norwegian girls resent the badge of service and I was no exception. I often stuffed the offensive cap in the breadbasket or cupboard, but Miss Lange supervised me with a ferret's eye. She appeared spinning the missing cap on her finger and waited while I put it on my head.

Juggling the soup bowls, I pushed my way out through the dining room door.

"Please hurry with the fish, Ragna," Mrs. Morrison prompted. "We don't wish to eat it cold."

That did it.

"Have you told them you have only one servant?" I hissed in Norwegian.

"Ragna! I will talk with you later."

Normally the ladies were patient with my mistakes. Learning English on the job provided some golden opportunities for confusion. When the window cleaner arrived, I gave him a brown paper package containing shoes to be polished and sent him away despite a barrage of unintelligible protest. One day, I seated a guest in the parlour and offered him some taffy. "Please wait, sir. I will call Miss Lange." I heard a small shriek when she entered the room. The visitor turned out to be a beggar. Miss Lange taught me to ask in English, "Are you a guest?"

While my mistresses traveled in Italy, I worked several weeks for another family. As one of seven servants, I became a chambermaid. One morning one of the three maiden sisters refused her breakfast tray. I sympathized, "Oh, you have trouble in your belly." I received a stern lecture on the use of the word "stomach."

The weather grew so warm I had to remove my uniform cap. I was chided for it. Even the parakeet, the mistresses pet, joined in, scolding me every time I neared its cage. "Who is it? Who is it," the parakeet screeched each time someone came to the door. "Oh, be quiet," I screeched back. I reddened the first time the parakeet shrieked at the mistress, "Oh, be quiet, Oh, be quiet."

Each morning I served my employers the gardener's ripe strawberries in a fine crystal bowl. I watched as they poured heavy cream from a silver pot, to drown the red-red berries in white. I coveted those strawberries. Had they left one behind, I would have gobbled it up, but that never happened. The old ladies liked strawberries too.

One night, very late, I stole out to the garden. I would eat one strawberry. No one would miss one strawberry. I lifted the net and ate one. Then another. I plucked one strawberry from this plant, two from another, but not enough from any section to make the gardener suspicious. Gloriously sated, I tiptoed back to my room.

Next morning, the gardener stood in the kitchen, talking with the butler and chauffeur.

"Did you enjoy your strawberries?" he called out.

The others turned. I felt my face grow hot.

"Strawberries? What are you talking about?"

"I say your foot prints, Miss. Knew right away it was you. English girls have small feet."

I fled from the kitchen. Luckily, Tuesday was my day off. Let the strawberry incident blow over. I would be off exploring London, perhaps Hyde Park, perhaps sipping tea at the Scandinavian Club. The kind Mrs. Morrison had searched out this simple clubroom, where girls from Sweden, Denmark and Norway met on their free days. I made a friend there, Christina, a pretty Danish girl who spoke excellent English. She taught me many new expressions. We were together on November 11 when the whole of London stopped to honor Armistice Day. Cabs, machines, buses, everything stopped for two minutes. My friend and I were amazed. One day, Christina failed to appear for our weekly tea together. A Swedish girl told me her story. She and a friend had spent an afternoon in the park. They parted to take different buses home. An old lady approached Christina at the bus stop and asked the girl to kindly help her across the street. Just as they reached the opposite curb, Christina saw her bus coming and ran back across the street. She stepped on the bus, reached for her change and collapsed.

Christina woke up in a London hospital with a police inspector in her room. Answering his questions, she described helping the elderly woman. The inspector informed Christina that a man, a white slave trader, had disguised himself as the "old lady" Christina assisted. Christina remembered a small prick in her arm. She learned that if the bus had not arrived at a lucky moment, she might have fallen victim to a vicious white slave kidnaping operation.

This harrowing experience kindled the writer in me to action. I wrote an article, "Big City Danger" and sent it to the Steinkjer newspaper. They published it and a series of others. My parents began to request my return home. But *Mor* admitted that hardly a dry eye remained in Steinkjer when people read "My First Christmas in a Strange Land."

My own free days offered adventure. One morning I set out for Hyde Park, still new enough to be enchanted by its Flower Walk and tea gardens, model boats on Round Pond, singers, mandolin players and wild-eyed politicians at Speakers Corner. I had fun riding on the top floor of the double decker bus. After a small lunch, I watched a group of happy children at play. I strolled by the carousel. I had a photo of myself wearing my new Panama hat, astride a prancing wooden steed. Suddenly, my eye caught a familiar face. A teacher from the Steinkjer school. And his new wife. *Mor* had written that the two teachers had just married. I watched as shock crossed the young husband's face. "Ragna Opdahl, *God dag!* What in the world are you doing alone in public?" I didn't slow down. "Give my love to everyone," I called, waving as I passed. I knew my unmaidenly conduct would be the talk of Steinkjer. I didn't care.

Mrs. Burton, the cook, warned me not to go out alone. It was improper and dangerous, she said. "I am not afraid," I retorted. I continued to go alone, but I found myself unnerved by one circumstance. Negro men and dark Spaniards or Arabs stared at me. My white-blond hair and pale eyes were an oddity even in fair-haired London. One swarthy male in particular frightened me. I noticed him in the park and escaped to a tea place near Serpentine Lane. He came in. Later, he appeared behind me on the footpath. When I went to see the forest view, he stood nearby. A British man noticed my distress and spoke to me, pretending to be a friend.

Since the hour grew late this Tuesday, I steered myself toward the nearby Hyde Park exit. When I emerged from the park, I could not find the bus stop. The buildings looked unfamiliar. I had naively supposed that the park had only one exit.

I searched for my little map. I had forgotten both the map and my address book at home. I looked back at the park. A labyrinth of pathways criss-crossed the huge green space. I had wandered carelessly, probably far from my customary exit. What could I do now, with dark approaching? Surely not try to go back through the park?

A policeman passed. He tried to help me. I repeated one name: "Putney Bridge," feeling like a helpless fool. The officer escorted me to a subway station. I had never dared to ride the Tube. Over the roar of the trains, he shouted for me to get off at the third stop. Panic rose as I stood alone in that crowd awaiting the strange underground railway. I could not make myself understood well enough to ask a question. I forced myself to get on the car and exit at the suggested stop. In the fog that shrouded the intersection outside the station I tried to push down my confusion. I had the sinking sensation that now I was really lost. Where was I?

Finally, I began to recognize buildings. I hurried home to my little rented room and snatched up my address book. I never again left without it.

I spent very little money on my outings because I saved every shilling until I had enough to make a much-needed visit to a dentist. Mrs. Morrison recommended an elderly gentleman she had used for many years. I tapped on the office door and a vigorous young man swung the door wide. I stared. I expected a grandfather. Here stood a handsome young man, his amused smile as white as his jacket. I blushed to my stomach.

"I come wrong place, *ja*? No Doctor Treadwell?"

"I'm sorry for the confusion. I am Doctor Treadwell's partner. Please come in."

Jack Powell proved himself an able dentist. I explained that I had come to England to learn the language and to write.

"Ah, a writer. You must see the palace then, the Changing of the Guard. And visit Fleet Street and Trafalgar. Perhaps you would allow me to escort you one afternoon?"

We agreed to meet on Sunday. I had given up going to church. I had attended church in London only once. I walked toward the front and picked a seat where I could see and hear well. An elderly couple approached my pew and glared at me. I quickly slid over. But they walked away. It turned out that they went to summon the church servant. He asked me to move to the benches in the back. Everyone stared. I was humiliated. Servants must sit in the back on hard wooden benches while the wealthy enjoy reserved pews. Why do the English distinguish between rich and poor in God's house?

Jack Powell filled in my Sundays with London sightseeing and tea in wonderful places. He invited me to the cabaret, my first evening entertainment. I was nervous and excited. He had to ask my landlady's permission to keep me out past 10 p.m. I spent everything I had on an elegant new gown, but my choice proved wrong. The cabaret in Soho was casual. Jack suggested I wear my coat through the meal. The lamb chops were raw and had to be sent back. The music and dancing made up for everything. It was a wonderful evening. It looked to me like the beginning of a wonderful friendship.

While I was out with Jack, Mrs. Morrison became sick. Her doctor rushed her to the hospital. She died there. Miss Lange announced plans to sell everything and move back to Norway. Did I wish to come?

My life changed overnight. I no longer had a sponsor in England. But my friend, Karin, whom I met at the Scandinavian Club, had asked me to join her in France. She had recently obtained a position there. I wrote her immediately. She answered right away and offered her flat until I found a job and lodgings. I felt a pang writing my farewell note to Jack.

It was 1925. I, Ragna Opdahl, from a little town no one had heard of in Norway, had purchased a ticket to Paris, the city of romance, the cultural capital of the world. Who could predict what would happen next?

Chapter

Bed of Roses

Ah! A seat by the window. I maneuvered my bag and packages along the train's narrow aisle. I had only a little suitcase--a servant in uniform needs little in the way of clothes. "Excuse me, excuse me," I apologized in my careful English. I dropped into the plush chair exhausted, letting my packages for Karin tumble into my lap. Packing for Miss Lange's move to Norway and arranging my own trip to Paris demanded late nights and early mornings, with hard work and countless errands in between. Miss Lange finally departed in what looked like a troop movement of trunks, crates, boxes and luggage. She gave me a few crowns as a bonus and hugged me like a daughter--a most un-Miss Lange thing to do. She would sail today to Christiania. Oh, I *must* remember to say "Oslo." Over a year had passed since 1924 when my countrymen had changed the old Danish name, Christiania, to the new "Oslo." I was happy that Norwegian nationalists had demanded and gotten a Norwegian name for the capital.

The train lurched from Victoria Station and traveled through a part of London I had never seen, the grimy streets of teeming cockney neighborhoods, and on into the countryside. I was lulled by the uninterrupted sound of the wheels on the track as the Paris Express sped through England's pastoral landscape. Drugged by the rhythm, I fell into a heavy sleep.

I awoke later with a jolt. Something was wrong. I fought to rouse myself, but the heaviness of sleep lay leaden on me like *Farmor*'s thick winter quilt. It was the sound. No more music of metal rotating on metal. I heard the muffled hum of a motor and the shush-shush of water, a sound familiar to one raised on the fjord.

I glanced around. No one shared my distress. A man read a French newspaper by the train's gas lamp. A woman held her sleeping child. Two young men, students by the look of their book bags, talked insistently in low-toned French.

Have I boarded the wrong train? How did my passenger car get aboard a boat? Is this a dream?

The mother looked kind. "*Parlez vous Anglais?*" I asked her. She gave me a bewildered look. "Where are we?" I blurted, first in Norwegian, then in English. I must have spoken my English hastily. No one understood. The businessman turned to me and explained something in French, which sounded like the squabble of a fast-playing gramophone recording. I was lost.

I tried to control my fear. At sea on an unknown ocean enroute to an unknown destination, I felt helpless and completely alone. I sat awake during the darkest part of the night, my mind racing with scenarios of horror... the rail car highjacked by desperadoes... white slave kidnapping... trapped in a strange port at 3 a.m...

The other passengers slept. A gray pre-dawn revealed shadowy outlines of a ship's rail outside my window, with water beyond. Then as the light grew, land appeared. We docked. Everything came clear to me. The entire passenger car had crossed a small sea or lake aboard some kind of barge. Amid shouts of workers, the rail car rolled from what I learned later was a ferry onto track and connected with loud clanking to a French train. A French conductor came aboard. What sea lay between England and France? I despaired my lack of interest in geography. Of course. The English Channel. I felt like a fool. I had exhausted myself with worry. Every detail that appeared so dreadful in the dark after midnight seemed perfectly reasonable in the morning light.

An ominous cloud bank began to release a downpour. I could barely make out the streets and squares as we pulled into Paris. Surprised when the train came to an abrupt halt, I scurried to gather my things. There stood Karin, smiling under a huge black umbrella and waving a bright Norwegian flag. She chattered all the way to her flat, describing the city, her job, her French sweetheart. I felt so sleepy, I could hardly listen. Karin went into another room to find a picture of her young man. When she returned, she found me asleep.

Within a few days I found a job as governess to a family outside Paris with three boys, ages eight, six and four. The mother spoke English, so I understood my orders and could report on the children's activities. The father and sons spoke French, and the little

I loved being a governess, but longed to taste the glamour of glittering 1920s Paris.

boys taught me their language. People praised my accent. We had lively times together, doing lessons at home with the boys laughing and correcting my pronunciation. We skated on a little lake in winter and roamed the French countryside in summer.

I joined Karin's French class on our day off. I met several Norwegian girls. Sometimes we all met in Paris to see a movie. Because the French spoke quickly and peppered their talk with idioms, I preferred the American silent pictures. Rudolph Valentino became my hero. Mary Pickford charmed us all. Friends began to say that I looked like Bette Davis. Karin repeated this to her boyfriend, urging him to find a friend for me. "Don't bother trying to find me a beau," I protested. "I would rather stay home and write."

My young charges behaved well. I loved my work with them, but the glitter of Paris life did not extend beyond the city's boundaries. I dreamed of strolling the *Avenue du Bois de Boulogne* in a chemise like the flapper I had seen in a French fashion magazine. I dared myself to smoke a cigarette in a Left Bank cafe. In Steinkjer, the townfolk labeled women who smoked as hussies, or worse. But Steinkjer was miles and years behind me. Fashionable Parisian women smoked. It looked sophisticated. I inhaled the first draught boldly, then dissolved into a very unsophisticated coughing fit when the smoke first slammed into my lungs. I learned to take little puffs and soon became quite adept at smoking.

Paris in the 1920s dazzled the world. The American expatriate writers, Hemingway and Fitzgerald, were popping champagne corks in the bar of *Le Trou dans le Mur* or the Ritz. Pablo Picasso and Georges Roualt debuted their paintings in neighborhood galleries. Although I knew none of these people, I followed every mention of France's cultural heroes in the newspaper. The excitement of it went to my head, leaving me as giddy as the cigarette smoke. I daydreamed about seeing the Riviera. I was an aspiring writer. I yearned to live the life of the famous writers I read about.

I believe that is why I accepted the Greek's invitation. I met him at *Chez les Vikings*, a bar in Paris where my friends and I liked to go. We drank Pernod and watched people there. The Greek said he was a journalist who had come to Paris to research the city's bistros and clubs. I told him that I too was a writer and was looking for material for my articles which were published in several Oslo magazines. The Greek invited me to come with him to the *Cafe des Amateurs* the next week and then on to some bistros on the Left Bank. I was excited and scared.

"This blonde hair and pale look must go," he told me. "They will think you a spy." He hinted of opium and cocaine in the places we would visit. "You must look *Francaise*." He sent me a black wig. I made up my face and dressed myself like a French *poivrotte*, which is a female drunkard. I looked nervously in the mirror before I left. A slash of brilliant red at the lips, penciled brows, black mascara. My skirt barely covered my thighs. I had fixed my blouse to make a plunging neckline and tied a black scarf on the wig.

Most of the people in the first place were drunk on cheap wine. The airless cave reeked with the sour smell of drunkenness and the stink of unwashed bodies. I began to feel less nervous and somewhat disgusted. In several places, people smoked opium through Chinese pipes. I couldn't talk to the Greek over the noise and the barrier of our second-language French. I found I disliked the Greek anyway. I went with him three or four times, but never wrote about my experiences. The gaudy descent into the city's low life made me feel dirty. What I wanted was a glimpse of Parisian elegance--quite beyond the reach of a young immigrant stuck in the French countryside in domestic service.

If I hadn't given up on religion, I would have said my prayers were answered. My friend mentioned an Argentine family in Paris that needed a nurse for a three-month old baby. They preferred a nurse willing to travel, for they planned a European tour the following spring. My two-year agreement with the French family expired soon. I was intoxicated with the hope of getting this position. I waltzed around my tiny *chambre* with a pillow singing in Norwegian at the top of my lungs until the little boys came running to see if I had gone mad. I telephoned my Norwegian friend to ask for more details on the job. "You are an optimist," she teased. "Don't get all hotheaded. The family insists on a Catholic nurse and probably prefers someone who speaks Spanish. You're crazy to think about it."

"I never look on the dark side," I told her sweetly and rang off. I wanted the job. Among my references I had a letter from Inga, a mid-wife in Norway I had assisted. The letter praised my skills as a baby nurse. I contacted the Argentine man, Senor Carlo, for an appointment.

A week later I floated through the crowd on the *Boulevard St.-Germain*. He liked me! Senor Carlo hired me on the spot, Catholic or no Catholic, because he and his young wife, Elsa, liked me. I smiled at people on the street. The salary doubled my income and the housekeeper had measured me for a smart new uniform--dress, cape, coat, veil, everything. They planned a trip to the south of France in March, then to Spain for Easter and Switzerland in May.

The young wife--less than 20 I imagined--had settled the issue. "The baby is only three months old," she reminded her husband. "The nurse's religion will not matter, only that she is loving and capable. Later, when Phillipo is older, we shall have a Catholic governess."

Senora Carlo had shiny hair, black as a crow's wing, and huge dark-blue eyes set against ivory skin. She looked so fragile, I wondered that she could bear a child. When she reasoned in her quiet, gentle voice, her husband's resistance melted.

Older than Elsa, probably around thirty, Senor Carlo worked as an engineer for an Argentine company's Paris office. He drove a large Mercedes. Before my uniform fitting I watched him leave to return to his business. He looked handsome driving away, his glossy

dark hair, brown eyes and white teeth emphatic above an im-
peccable white collar. In England I had met people who were rich,
but Senor Carlo was the first young rich person I had encountered.
Both he and his wife fascinated me. They had glamour. I called
them my "Aristocrats".

I caught snatches of the city on my days off during the months
to come. I was happy to escape to the outdoors and stretch my legs
on the gravel paths of the *Jardin du Luxembourg*. The wind had
stripped the last leaves from the park's trees. Their sculptured outlines stood stark against the sky. Clumps of leaves, sodden from
Paris' cold autumn rains, lay brown against the fading grass.

I enjoyed the tap-tap of my new black shoes against the shimmering wet pavement as I passed the shops crowded along the street.
They bunched together like eager children squeezing to fit in a
school photograph. On fine days, their doors remained open to se-
duce my nostrils with the smell of their wares. The enticing scents
from the herb-seller, the siren aroma of fresh bread at the *boulan-
gerie*, the elegant fragrance from the *perfumier*. But today all the
doors were closed. It felt good to go inside to warmth and misted
windows. I decided to save the booksellers along the quais on the
windswept Seine for another day.

After the rains came the clear, cold weather and some snow.
When the weather warmed enough for Phillipo to ride in his carriage, my mistress advised me to begin preparations for the family's
spring tour. She ordered sun hats for little Phillipo and light cotton
shirts for Senor Carlo. The luggage came down from the attic. A
messenger delivered a portfolio of tickets. With each step my anticipation grew. This trip satisfied my wildest fantasies: Travel to the
pleasure capitals of 1920s Europe... Nice, Cannes, Monte Carlo.

We drove in the Mercedes to the French Riviera and rented a
house. Not a house, a castle. The franc had fallen so low, I discovered, that Argentine money bought the privileges of wealth. The
Carlo family provided amply for my needs. They made certain I received the best food in the resort hotels. They ordered the finest ac-
commodations for me. I had only to ring for my dinner. A maid
pressed my uniform and turned down my bed. For the first time, I
tasted ease. I had never experienced the sense of harmony that
comes with luxury and leisure. I fell right into it. It was fun to pre-
tend alone in my *chambre* that I was born to a life of ease but sometimes I felt guilty. I ate my tournedos and thought of *Mor* stirring a
pot of rye porridge at home.

Senor Carlo hired a chauffeur in Nice. He drove us along the *Av-*

enue des Anglais to the fancy stores and past the casinos. Nice swarmed with people of all nationalities and languages. I made friends with Pierre, the chauffeur, and his wife. We talked of the casinos, where fashionable people from all over Europe and America gambled in the evening. "Oh, how I would like to be dressed up and go dancing there!" I confided to Pierre. "No sooner said than done," he exclaimed. "I will arrange it."

A few nights later, I was dancing with a young Frenchman Pierre brought along, whirling like a princess in one of my childhood folk tales. Pierre took my hand later for a waltz. "No one knows we are servants," he whispered with a wink. I didn't mind my Cinderella story. Next morning I rose early with Phillipo, full of energy.

At first my Aristocrats seemed stiff, but when they saw how I cared for their sweet baby they began to like me. One day Senor Carlo invited me to join him, Senora Carlo, her sister and her mother, who were both traveling with us, to visit a museum. Perhaps I would see a Cezanne painting, I thought as I dressed for the outing. The museum displayed no art. Instead one toured the halls to view instruments of torture from Inquisition days. I flinched at the first, a device that pulled off a heretic's toenails. Those who disputed the religious hierarchy of the day, Jews and other unbelievers, had their toes trimmed off, their sinews stretched to snapping on a rack, their bodies publicly burned at the stake.

The museum air stood still, fetid and musty. I felt myself gasping for breath and getting none. Experts in the art of torture had ripped prisoners' bodies apart with these very machines--in the name of religion. I turned in the dim light of an interior chamber and stumbled into a hall. The museum became a maze. I hurried through hallways and suites of rooms filled with instruments of horror. Finally, I glimpsed light and plunged down a stairway into the shimmering radiance of the Mediterranean seaside. Sinking onto a bench beneath a leafy canopy, I gulped the fresh air and wondered: Who was the God of the Inquisition? What God did these people seek to serve?

These questions and images melted from my mind under the balmy sunshine. We fell into a rhythm of seaside life--bathing in the Mediterranean, lunch, an outing and a rest before dinner. Everyone felt rested by the time we left the beautiful Cote d'Azur for Spain. We enjoyed the tiny towns, overflowing with flowers, along the route to southern Spain. Everyone relaxed, except Phillipo, who possessed the energy and consuming curiosity of a baby who has just learned to crawl.

Seville made an impact on me that I shall never erase from my memory. Spain is a land of extremes and Seville a city of extremes. The balmy grace of its sunny clime covered a violence embroiled by the relentless sun. An opulent church overlaid with silver and gold towered to the heavens while street people squatted in its shadow combing and picking lice from one another's hair... a man who drove donkeys all day on the arrastre for eighty cents in wages... a procession of *penitentes* bearing heavy crosses that rubbed the skin raw. For the three days before Easter the crowds sobbed and wailed at the processions, their brown eyes flowing tears. I thought of Norway's people, their ice-blue eyes, their passionless reserve.

During one of the *penitente* walks, a man stopped in the procession and stared at me. "*Linda rubia*," he breathed, almost in reverence. His words meant "beautiful blonde." Then he threw down his cap and gestured for me to step on it. I retreated into the press of people. He cast me a stricken look, as if his heart were broken. His eyes were eloquent. I was embarrassed.

A few days after Easter, we gathered for the highlight of our time in Spain, the bullfight. We walked to the arena through Seville's narrow streets, arriving early for the five o'clock event. The Spanish mood was festive, the stands overflowing with joyous fans. Their shouting would have made my proper Mrs. Morrison cringe.

"Where is the bull kept?" I asked Senor Carlo. He explained that the bull must be angry to give the patrons a good show. Therefore, the Spanish shut the bull in a dark enclosure and withheld food for several days before the bullfight. When the matador strode to the center of the field to receive the crowd's roar of praise, the animal handlers drove a needle into the bull's thick neck. It made the bull wild with pain. The gate opened and the crazed bull emerged into the dazzling sunlight, blinded by brightness and startled by the noise of the crowd. Then the contest began.

I had spent my childhood caring for animals. I was upset by Senor Carlo's story. But I could not ask more because the music of the *paso doble* began. The matador, in a heavily embroidered silk jacket and skin-tight pants, marched into the ring, followed by his assistants, the *bandilleros* and the *picadores*.

The frenzy of the crowd rose as the matador began to flaunt his cape before the bull, whipping the animal's anger from plateau to plateau of rage. His straight, proud back, his deft ballet passes, his imperious control both fascinated and repelled me.

I listened to my Aristocrats talk. I was beginning to understand

Spanish. The first series of maneuvers with the cape they called *veronicas,* named for the woman who offered a cloth to Christ on his way to Calvary.

The mounted *picadores* rode into the ring bearing lances. I noticed the shine of their silver jackets and the equally brilliant glare of their steel leg armor. The horses distracted the snorting animal. The matador worked to recapture his attention. Suddenly, the bull charged one of the riders. The *picadore* showed his skill, guiding his mount to avoid the attack. The bull paused. The arena fell silent. And then, in what seemed like slow motion, the bull lowered his horns and charged again. The *picadore*'s horse reared and came down. To my horror, I saw his belly impaled on the brutal horns of the bull. Blood spurted everywhere. The *picadore* tumbled off like an acrobat and escaped. The bull continued to gore the horse.

I screamed, a high-pitched terrible scream lost amid the shouts of the crowd. I clambered over my employers. "Excuse me, please. I must leave." I tried not to offend. An American woman, smoking a cigarette and staring at the bloody scene below, blocked my way until I got her attention. I did not wish to go back, but I wondered what Senor Carlo would think of me. When I finally returned to my seat, the matador was bowing low in the ring, accepting a hero's honor. Senor Carlo apologized for the distressing incident with the horse. I decided to ask him the question on my mind. "Why didn't the horse scream? I heard nothing."

"This may sound cruel to you," he replied. "But the Spanish anticipate this kind of unpleasant accident. So, they cut the horse's vocal cords before the animals are allowed to enter the ring."

I became nauseous.

Caught in a happy moment between my mistress' death and Alfredo's, I walk a French boulevard with an eager Phillipo and a shy Elcita.

A Paris photographer captured my emerging sophistication. The next few years would provide my first taste of tragedy.

Chapter

Wooed and Widowed

I found I could not eat. I lost weight over the next weeks. When I wrote a letter to *Far* before leaving Spain, I tried not to remember the horse. I only said, "I have seen my first bullfight. I found it brutal. How can people condone this in a Christian country?"

After the bullfight, my emotions took a tailspin. I would go to bed hating the dusky complexions, the underlying brutality of Spain. I dreamed of the bloody horse. Then next morning, I would pull Phillipo in his wagon to the park and feel happy. My nightmare seemed remote. Young students from the University nearby smiled at me and said, "Hello, Miss" thinking that my light blue uniform meant I was English. I watched the palm trees swaying in the sea breeze. Seville's flowers bloomed everywhere. I met a nice young man, Alberto, who invited me to a movie the next evening. While we talked, the baby began to fuss, so Alberto gave him a huge ring of keys to clatter. Phillipo banged the keys delightedly. We continued our talk in the shade of a cypress. Phillipo fell asleep. Finally, Alberto and I shook hands and said goodbye. Later, I discovered the young man's keys in the baby's wagon. I hoped he could wait until tomorrow night for their return. That evening, Senora Carlo asked me to pack. We would leave for Madrid in the morning. "Oh!," I said, "so quickly?"

"Is this a problem for you, Ragna?"

"Oh, no! It's just. . . nothing."

I left the keys at the hotel's front desk with a message of apology. We drove to dark Madrid.

I received an inferior room in the Madrid hotel. No matter, but I felt wary when the waiter lingered in my room after serving my dinner. He looked too long at me. I felt uncomfortable. Of course, I had become accustomed to stares. My blonde head stood out like an exclamation point in the crowd. The reverse was true in Norway. When the gypsies, with their raven hair, came to Steinkjer, people paused in the street to stare. Little children ran after them calling "porkey, porkey," which I now realized was a repeat of the gypsies' *por qui*? I understood the stares, but I would never understand the passion, the heat, the turbulence in these Spanish men.

In the night I heard a noise at my door. Someone was forcing the flimsy bolt. The intruder began beating on the door and pleading in Spanish. The waiter! I pushed a heavy dresser in front of the door. I was bathed in perspiration, trembling. When he left, I did not sleep. I wanted to leave Spain. Behind the fragrance of its summer flowers lay the sinister scent of violence.

Phillipo's grandmother shared my feeling. She disliked Madrid and persuaded Senor Carlo to take us on to Switzerland. We drove through France and Italy to get there. Almost at the border crossing, I felt the gloom lift from me. The border officials were calm and friendly. The guardian Alps towering overhead steadied me. Blue lakes and waterfalls smiled from the countryside.

Servants lined the walkway to greet us as we approached the large, comfortable house that became home for the next three months. Lake Leman (some call it Lake Geneva) was nearby, a wonderful place to stroll, fish or go boating. Phillipo and I enjoyed the cool summer weather. Everyone loved Switzerland.

One evening I found Senor Carlo pouring over maps in the library. He looked upset. "Is anything wrong, sir?" I asked. "We will return to Paris as quickly as possible," he answered, looking up from penciling a route. "Senora Carlo is ill."

We hurried to Paris, with my pale mistress unable to eat, nauseated by the motion of the automobile. She had experienced some hemorrhaging. I looked at my own strong hands. Her hand lay limp beside her. I feared for my little mistress for she had so little stamina. When we reached Paris, the doctor informed Elsa Carlo that a baby was coming. After a few weeks of rest, Senora Carlo revived. She now looked forward happily to the baby's birth. "I am so sorry I dragged everyone home from Switzerland," she said, her blue eyes apologetic. "That country is the most beautiful I have seen."

"Ah, but you have not seen Norway," I replied. "Picture the Alps cut by deep fjords, so deep whales swim there, so clean they reflect the snow-capped peaks like a mirror."

"You are a poet," my mistress teased. But she caught my enthusiasm for Norway.

We all talked of Norway then. My Aristocrats planned a trip to Scandinavia as soon as the new baby grew big enough to travel. At night, after I put Phillipo to bed, I visualized our sojourn. Home! How much I missed my family! How I appreciated my beautiful Norway now that I had seen the world.

I awoke one night to the noise of footsteps and excited voices in the hall. The baby has come, I thought. Light shone beyond my door. Phillipo's grandmother was outside my room in night clothes. A beautiful baby girl had arrived, she told me. The doctor had just finished, but a nurse would stay on with mother and baby. I could take Phillipo in to see his new sister in the morning.

The little one had red hair and her mother's startling dark blue eyes. Her face looked like a rosebud, fresh and fair. I heard flapping steps behind and turned to encounter Elsa's nurse. My jaw dropped. Her uniform bore stains from many days service. Her unkempt hair needed washing. The flop-flop came from a soiled pair of slippers. I scooped up the infant. "I am the baby nurse," I said, glaring at the woman. "I will take the baby to the nursery."

"*Attendez! Le bebe doit rester ici!*" she protested.

I shut my ears and strode down the hall to the spotless sanctuary of the nursery with Phillipo clutching my skirt behind me. Had I overstepped my bounds? The thought flashed through my anger. I did not care. I refused to allow that slovenly woman to lay a hand on the newborn. I would bring the baby to Senora Carlo to nurse, no matter what the hour.

The family let me keep the baby in the nursery. But young Elsa did not regain her strength. She lay listless in bed, barely able to rouse herself to feed her daughter. Then she developed a fever, soon a raging fever. Her tongue became bright red and a rash erupted on her chest. Her breasts swelled painfully. I had to find a wet nurse, for the Senora could no longer take the child. The doctor gave Senor Carlo his diagnosis: Scarlet fever.

She never improved. The fever consumed my little mistress. Her fragile body, weakened by childbirth, succumbed quickly. She was gone before we knew to say goodbye, dead at twenty-one.

Senor Carlo went wild with grief. He refused to eat. At night we heard him wandering the house sleepless. The shock and pain to all of us cannot be described. We learned the careless nurse had come to our home from tending scarlet fever patients. I watched Phillipo's grandmother, afraid that she could lose her mind. Her hair grayed before our eyes in a matter of weeks. My little Phillipo looked at me with his sweet eyes puzzled and asked for his Mama. His plaintive question became a knife entering my heart.

Why did God allow this to happen? These were kind, good people, a loving happy family, so full of life. Death had poisoned each one, sure as a serpent's tongue flashing out to pierce the tender flesh of a young child. Life and goodness left our home.

We mourned. My mistress' body was embalmed and sent to Argentina. I cared for the two little ones. Dark months passed. I could escape the pervading sense of grief when I took the babies for an airing in the park. There we played and laughed in the sunshine. Sometimes, Alfredo, Senor Carlo's friend, came to the nursery to play with the children after visiting the family. He liked to talk with me. He helped to brighten our days.

The family talked of returning to Argentina. I could understand their Spanish now, although they didn't suspect that and spoke freely in front of me. They talked about my coming with them to South America. But I would have to become a Catholic, they agreed. Senor Carlo called me to his study.

"We would like you to meet our French priest, Ragna. You may have some questions about our Catholic religion. As you know, we are planning to return to Argentina. When we go, we would like to take you with us. But Phillipo is growing and will need instruction in his faith. Do you understand what I am saying?"

I understood and I agreed to talk with the priest. After Spain I had plenty of questions for him.

I rode the trolley to the church where the priest had his office. I almost lost my courage as my hollow footsteps echoed against the soaring vaulted ceiling of *Saint-Eustache*. Outside, the tumultuous market, *Les Halles*, clamored with vendor's shouts, music and rumbling horse-drawn wagons. But inside the Gothic sixteenth-century church of *Saint-Eustache*, silence stood like a presence.

I felt like an ant, toiling my way to the front of the nave, dwarfed by sheer distance and the colossal proportions of the ornate pillars, the columns and the great arcades. *Saint-Eustache* is almost as big as Notre Dame. Its grandness borders on the theatrical. All the power of the Renaissance church seemed to be focused in this one space. Its profuse decoration both fascinated and threatened me. By the time I reached the altar to meet the priest, I was perspiring.

His black robes rustled as he led me down several hallways to a small office where he motioned me to a chair in front of his desk.

He talked about Christ who founded the church. ("Thou art Peter and upon this rock I will build my church.") He talked about the Pope, the Eucharist, the Mass, the Rosary. I listened, no longer overwhelmed. When he paused, I almost jumped in with my questions.

"What happens when we die?"

I found the Catholics believe in hell.

"Is there a devil? Could a good God have created an evil being to serve Him?"

"Is there burning fire in hell? Could the rich pay for prayers and thus get to heaven quicker? What about the injustice of rich and poor in Catholic countries like Spain? What about the Inquisition? What about. . .?"

The priest was shaking his head. He glanced at a pocket watch and I could see the interview was over.

A few days later Senor Carlo spoke to me and explained that the family would find a Catholic nurse in Argentina. I understood that he had talked to the priest. I felt sad as I helped to prepare the children's things for the voyage.

Alfredo visited more often now. He too worked as an engineer for the Argentine firm and carried papers back and forth to Senor Carlo. He spent many afternoons in the nursery. One day he asked me to go with him to see the flowering trees in the *Jardin des Tuileries.*

I felt myself blush. He was very kind, I explained, but I understood my position in the household. I could not go. He was frank. He said that my being a governess did not matter to him. He enjoyed my company and would like to see me on my days off. His determination surprised me. He seemed reserved, yet he would go after what he wanted.

I met Alfredo at the *Tuileries* beneath the *Arc de Triomphe du Carrousel.* We became so absorbed in conversation that we barely saw the sights. I remember his beautiful manners. Despite my humble background and my present station, Alfredo treated me like a baroness. I had never trusted a man since Reidar but I began to trust Alfredo.

My Argentine family planned to sail in two weeks. Alfredo asked me what I wanted to do when they left.

"I don't know. Look for another position, I suppose." The truth was that I didn't want to think about their departure. The babies were like my own.

Alfredo's gaze penetrated.

"Ragna, I believe it is time to talk about the future, the future for you and me."

I couldn't believe what I saw in his eyes.

He took my hands in his and looked into my eyes. "I love you. I would like to marry you."

Could this be happening to me? I looked on our romance as a fairy tale, the same kind of fairy tale as my dancing in the casino ballroom in Nice or pretending to be a wealthy heiress in a luxurious hotel on the Cote d'Azur. A dream. Dreams had to end. I looked into Alfredo's brown eyes and saw that he meant every word. I knew he was a man I could trust and love. I said yes.

It happened so quickly. I hugged my precious little ones for the last time and turned around to walk down the aisle of a French chapel. We kept the wedding ceremony simple. Karin, my two Norwegian friends now married to Frenchmen and a handful of Alfredo's friends helped us celebrate.

I found married life as fizzy as the wedding champagne. We laughed about a Norwegian bride cooking French food to suit an Argentinean. We made plans for the future, trips to Norway and South America to visit families, plans for our future home, our children. We spent our weekends outdoors. He enjoyed nature as much as I. While Alfredo worked, I kept house and found time for my writing again. I found he looked at the good side of people and situations. We were happy.

Almost two years after the wedding, I visited a doctor to confirm my suspicions that I was pregnant. Yes, a baby was on the way, *Monsieur le Docteur* informed me, due in the autumn.

I'll tell Alfredo tomorrow evening, after the theater, I decided. We'll come home to a late dinner beside the little fireplace and I will surprise him then.

I prepared an elegant supper, but Alfredo could not eat when we returned from the theater. He looked flushed. He said he had been sick in the men's room during the intermission but did not wish to spoil the evening for me. Would I excuse him now? He went to bed and vomited several times. After midnight, his temperature rose alarmingly. I helped him into his coat. There was a hospital nearby. The doctors there would know how to treat the fever.

At one o'clock in the morning the hospital bustled with activity. Sick people crowded the lobby. Attendants hurried back and forth. "Spanish influenza," one of them told me. "The hospital is full."

The glare of the lights made everything unreal. People came and went as if on motion picture film. The doctor came out and told me

Alfredo had the Spanish flu. It wasn't really happening somehow.

"How long must he stay then?" I asked.

"You can see for yourself, the hospital is overcrowded. If he improves, we'll be forced to send him home. Of course, the disease is highly contagious."

"What do you mean, *if* he improves?"

"Your husband is seriously ill, Madame. The fever is high, very high. We have no effective medicine for this influenza. But he is young and strong. You must pray, Madame."

Pray! I wanted to *do* something! I wanted to go into the influenza ward and sponge him to cool the fever. I wanted to make the doctors find a medicine. I wanted to get him out of this hospital where the doctors looked so hopeless and take him somewhere else for help. But they told me all the hospitals were overloaded.

I sat on a bench in my evening clothes all the next day. Alfredo grew worse. We talked a little, but he was delirious most of the day. In the evening, he lay spent by the fever, unable to talk to me. The nurses asked that I leave the ward. The flu struck everyone who came in contact with it, they warned me. I thought of the little life growing inside me. I stayed in the waiting room. In the early morning hours of the next day, the doctor found me there. Alfredo was dead.

No!

I tried to scream, but no sound came out. I did not cry. I was too stunned to respond with tears. I waited until dawn, then called Karin. She arranged the funeral. I remember the same faces as those at our wedding. The Catholic priest prayed in Latin. They shoveled dirt over Alfredo's coffin and the little stones made an empty sound as they tumbled onto the box. When the earth was smoothed over the grave, the rain-damp soil looked ready for planting. I had a strange desire to push seeds into the dirt. April is a cruel time, breeding pain and birth. I wondered if there is a God, if there is a resurrection. Was my beloved Alfredo dead, utterly and irrevocably dead? I thought about my baby, the tiny innocent child within me who had done nothing wrong and had already been punished by life. The two of us were forced to go on. I felt angry at God and even angry at Alfredo for leaving me and our baby. For the first time, in a mixture of grief, self-pity and rage, I cried. I got down on my knees and took a handful of death-life dirt in my hand. I squeezed it hard in my fist and let the tears come.

Freda's thin cheeks had plumped out under Tante Margit's care when we sat for this mother-daughter photo in 1933.

Chapter

New Vision

Spring's first leaves veiled the birch trees in light-green lace the day my train pulled into Steinkjer. My mother and father, brothers and sisters and many friends waved from the platform. On the way home, I heard the piercing call of the co-co bird and spotted the tiny blue and white flowers that bloom in the harsh mud that borders melting snowfields in May. *Mor* had baked a special cake to celebrate. Coffee fragrance filled the kitchen. I was home.

I cried on my mother's shoulder until there were no more tears. Then we prepared for my baby.

On September 25, 1931 I gave birth to a daughter and named her Freda, after her father. When Freda was only a few months old, *Mor* suffered a stroke. She never regained her speech. Soon after, my mother died.

All the pain of Alfredo's death returned and overlaid my grief at losing *Mor*. My heart ached for my father, lonely in the house empty without *Mor*. I wondered again about the resurrection. How could I believe in eternal life when I couldn't be sure there was a God? *Mor* had urged me to have the baby baptized. "If she died today, she would go to hell," she argued. To please my mother, I made a christening dress and took Freda to the *prest* to be baptized. I wanted to ask him if God would condemn an infant to hellfire. I needed the hope of seeing my loved ones again. But I couldn't overcome my distaste for the image of a punishing, vengeful God. Christmas passed in confusion and anguish.

I planned to take care of *Far* that winter. Instead I battled for my baby's life. Freda caught whooping cough when an epidemic hit Steinkjer. Many babies died. The local doctors told me that Freda's only chance to survive lay with the specialists in the Oslo children's hospital. In a blur of misery I took my sick baby on the train to Oslo. There the doctors found water filling Freda's tiny lungs. They needed to operate or my baby would suffocate.

I fell on my knees. "Oh, God," I prayed, "if you are real, help me. I have lost my husband and my dear mother. If I lose my little baby, I will have no reason to go on. Please let my baby live."

For days after the surgery, Freda slept. I winced when I saw the tubes coming out of her tiny chest. She had lost her baby plumpness and color. She looked as skinny and pale as a plucked bird. My heart sank when I saw her. "How is my baby?" I said to the nurse. "I wish we could tell you something else," she said. "We don't have much hope." I sat beside the bed. Every fiber of my being cried out, "Live! Live!" I spoke softly to her. I sang nursery songs, promised treats for when she got better--I would take her to the zoo to see the bears and she would have a little wagon. I believed and despaired and prayed. She slept.

On the fourth day, the lady doctor was finishing her examination when I returned to Freda's room from the head nurse's station. The nurse felt sorry for me and gave me a cup of coffee once in a while. "How is she?" I asked Margit, the doctor. "The same." I walked over to Freda and bent to kiss her curly head. I tickled her thin arm. "Mama's back now," I whispered.

My baby opened her brown eyes and looked at me. She gave me a weak smile.

Tears ran down my face. I looked over and saw the doctor crying and laughing. We became friends that day.

Margit, the doctor, was German, a distinguished-looking woman with swept-back brown-gray hair and kind blue eyes. She stood 5'6" or 5'7", slight but erect. Though we came from two different worlds--hers graced by family position and education--she treated me like a friend. She had a slight separation in her evenly-placed teeth and oversized ears, but she impressed me as dignified. Her strong, lean face showed smile lines around the eyes. I noticed her gentleness with my baby. I couldn't have hoped for a better doctor--or friend.

One of the nurses, Nancy, also became my friend. She listened to me during my baby's crisis hours. I'm afraid I stretched her patience, demanding how God could let sickness snatch an innocent baby. And if she were unbaptized, would she burn in hell? Why wars and dictators and murderers, if God was in charge?

After Freda passed the turning point, I spent the long night hours at the hospital talking with Nancy. She gave me a Bible and helped me to find answers to my questions in the Scriptures. Nancy read the story of Adam and Eve with me. God didn't make Freda ill," she told me. "We inherit sickness and death from Adam and Eve. But God sent Jesus to ransom us from the captivity of these things." She read me Jesus' words that compared death to sleep. I found no mention of my Sunday school teacher's burning hell or the tortured Purgatory of the Parisian priest.

I found myself hungry to read my new Bible. One passage excited me to read another. The Scriptures came alive. I ragged poor Nancy with questions. She gave me several books and tracts. They bore the name "International Bible Students." These books described the New World promised by Jehovah God through the prophet Isaiah. I learned that Jehovah Himself will one day rule the earth with righteousness and justice. Then all our suffering and death will be over. "The leopard will lie down with the goat... The young child will put his hand into the viper's nest." The Book of Revelation promises a new heaven and a new earth "and death shall be no more, neither shall there be mourning nor crying nor pain anymore, for the former things have passed away."

For the first time, a religious idea rang true for me. This kind of belief seemed right. My childhood faith was like a beautiful symphony played off key. I had wanted to listen, but all I heard were the discordant notes. The International Bible Students believed in the Bible's promise of a New Earth. Their talk rekindled my youthful dream of a new Eden-like world that would replace heaven as our reward for being good. That same vision that once angered my religion teacher and ended my Sunday school career, came alive again. I remembered a book in Miss Lange's library in London called *The Bible and Creation.* "May I read this one?" I had asked, excitement tingling in my voice. She took the book in her hand, turning its glossy pages, and shook her head. "You won't be able to understand it. It uses courtly language," she said. Disappointed, I took a book by Ibsen instead. But I couldn't shake the magnetism of the creation book. "It's a religious book, Ragna, about how God created the earth," Miss Lange explained, replacing the heavy volume on its shelf. I had not read the Old Testament Book of Genesis and knew little of creation. How I longed to learn all there was to know! Later in France, Karen had a beautiful book describing Creation but I had not yet learned to read French. All my yearning to discover how the world began, how evil entered the world and what was God's plan to restore mankind to righteousness was finally satisfied in the books Nancy gave me. Deception, sickness and death had crept on serpent legs into my own Eden. I mourned with Eve over the lifeless body of her son, Abel. I could read and understand these stories in my own Norwegian. I now had a firm hope in the beautiful earthly world waiting beyond the resurrection. I wanted to become an International Bible Student to share with others the good news I had found. Nancy invited me to go from house to house with her, to witness. I went. I felt like the disciples who met the resurrected Jesus on the road to Emmaus: "Are not our hearts burning within us, are not our hearts lighted with fire?"

My heart flamed. I felt called to witness. I saw Jehovah's hand in my life when Freda's doctor, whom we now called *Tante* Margit, asked if she might continue to nurse Freda in her home. "She is ready to leave the hospital but she needs constant care until she gets stronger," *Tante* Margit told me. Though my baby had passed her first birthday, she could not walk. She was delicate as a blown Easter egg shell, thin and pastel-pale. I had no home for her, just a cheap room with little light or air. *Tante* Margit spoke of her spacious house in pine-forested Holmenkollen, the crisp-air highlands overlooking Oslo.

"How can I thank you? It sounds wonderful for Freda! I will have time to find a place for us to live when she is completely well."

"I have grown fond of Freda," *Tante* Margit smiled. "You needn't thank me. I will be delighted to watch her grow strong."

I began witnessing full time. How scared I was! I knocked on my first door alone and when no one answered right away, I scurried off. "Wait," a woman called after me. "I am at home. You didn't give me time to get to the door."

"I'm helping some friends to pass out these booklets," I gulped. "Would you like one?" She took the booklet. At the second home, a woman gave me half a *kroner* to pay for a book and praised me for being a young person enthused about my religion. How foolish to be afraid, I told myself. Witnessing was easy.

Many people received my message. They accepted tracts and booklets from me. When I met my friends at day's end, the few witnessing in Oslo in those days, I had run out of printed handouts. They congratulated me. Flushed with success, I doubled my efforts. I wanted everyone to hear this wonderful news from the Bible.

Of course, people were hungry to read. Norway in the early 1930s had little in the way of entertainment. We read newspapers, but few people had radios. Norwegians devoured reading materials and treasured books. We International Bible Students, with our free pamphlets and books, fed a hunger among our countrymen.

I made just enough to keep food in my stomach by placing my books. When I went to visit Freda, *Tante* Margit asked me a startling question: Could she keep my Freda? She had remodeled a room to make a cheerful nursery. Freda had grown robust. She had learned to walk and run. She looked happy and at home with *Tante* Margit. The doctor talked about Freda's future--music lessons, skiing and sports, summer camp, schooling. I thought of my meager resources.

"But she is my child," I said. "I am the one who should raise her."

"She will remain your child," *Tante* Margit assured me. "I am not asking to adopt her. She will call you 'Mama' and me 'Tante.' Of course, you will visit her at any time. For as long as you desire, I will provide for her needs and daily care. She is yours to take back whenever you choose."

I could not deny the power of *Tante* Margit's argument. I almost hated her for being so reasonable. Freda would be better off in her care. I knew I was a good mother. If I took her back, she would have her own mother's love--but little else. I risked losing her love if I let her go. However, it began to look selfish to me to raise my own child under the circumstances--a woman alone with no real home or regular income. And the plain truth was that *Tante* Margit loved Freda too. Freda would have everything she needed. "I will consider it," I told Margit.

I telephoned a few days later and accepted her offer.

In some ways, I felt relieved. Financially, I had only myself to worry about and I could get by on nearly nothing. I began to broaden my witnessing activities, taking assignments in the countryside where I was happiest anyway. In winter, I combined my work with skiing in the splendid new snow, a nice reward for my labors. When my family called me home to Steinkjer to care for my father, I felt free to go. Though my little one could not withstand the harsh northern winter, she remained in *Tante* Margit's capable hands.

During the train ride, I realized I faced a challenge to my new faith. I found witnessing in Oslo easy. No one there knew me. The Bible instructs us to witness to the whole world. How would the people of Steinkjer accept this new message? I would begin with the Opdahls.

My father and *Mor*'s sister, *Tante* Louise, read my booklets. Before long, I hoped they would accept the truth. So! This prophet would not be despised in her own town. I went to my mother's friends. I sat drinking coffee and talking with *Fru* Torland, telling her about my life in London and Paris, my new work in Oslo. At first she seemed curious, then suspicious. To explain things better, I gave her the Watchtower magazine. She scanned the pages. "What's this?" she cried, pointing to a passage on death. "It's true, *Fru* Torland, we don't die at all, just sleep as Jesus said until the resurrection. *Mor* is not in heaven. She's waiting to rise and inhabit the New Earth."

"Blasphemy! Your mother is a saint in God's heaven today and you must not believe anything else."

"I don't believe she is in heaven. The Bible teaches that our heaven will be right here on earth. I don't think my mother would like a simpering, do-nothing heaven anyway. She'd rather be raising vegetables and baking bread for *Far* under Christ's perfect reign in the millenium."

"Ragna, Ragna, what rubbish! What have you come into? No heaven or hell? No eternal justice? This is a false, very false, religion!"

Her tirade came like a squally wind blasting me out of the house. I grabbed my things just before her scolding swept me through the door. I said "I'm sorry. I don't think you understand" until the door slammed shut behind me.

Fru Torland lost no time in lecturing my father about my "dangerous" views. "Ragna," he said, regarding me with sad eyes, "you will go to hell if you believe these things."

"*Far*, can't you see? There is no hell. God is love. He doesn't torture people. He loves them."

My father shook his head. Jens had entered the room but he said nothing. Jens had always supported me. I needed to count on him this time.

Jens continued to say nothing against my religion, until Christmastime, when he called me from the kitchen one afternoon.

"Look! I outdid myself this year. I believe this is the best Christmas tree we've ever had." I looked at the beautiful tree he had cut. He had already taken the Christmas boxes down from the closet. He began unwrapping the decorations that *Mor* had carefully packed away before her death. "Come, help me, Ragna. You and I will make this place look like Christmas!"

I shook my head.

"Come now. The pots and pans will wait. Here, hang this snowflake." He held out a crocheted ornament I had made as a child.

"No. I don't wish to decorate the tree, Jens. I don't believe in celebrating Christmas any more."

He looked at me in disbelief.

"The Bible doesn't say Jesus was born in December," I rushed to explain. "Christmas is a man-made custom. It was begun by pagans. So we don't celebrate."

I could see Jens was angry. He wouldn't turn around. "Please, try to understand," I pleaded. His neck had grown red and his shoulders took on a set I recognized. He began to hang ornaments with a fury.

No member of my family meant more to me than Jens. I thought of giving up. Why couldn't I just forget this new doctrine and help Jens with the tree? Then everything would be all right again. I went back into the kitchen, tears stinging my eyes. "I won't give up," I cried, beating my fist into the table. "I won't!" Jesus commanded his followers to forfeit father, mother or brother for him. Despite Jens I determined to continue. But my heart was broken for my brother alone in the next room.

The next day I strapped on my skis and settled my knapsack full of booklets on my back. I started south from Steinkjer into the farm district. The wind had blown hard off the North Sea all night, making a rigid ripple pattern on the snow crust, the way waves mark the sand. The wind had not quit. Out in the open, it stirred up snow ghosts. These whirlwind creatures rose up immense and menacing, advancing like angry spirits, then dissipating just before they could vent their blustery wrath on me. The snow made little nests that clung to crooks in the birch branches and I wondered that the wind didn't blow them away. The rounded mountains in the distance seemed coldly remote, wrapped in icy mystery.

I stopped at the first farmhouse. The people there listened to my message about the Kingdom and took my booklets. People around Steinkjer hung on my words about a Christ-governed world with no Hitler and no Nazis, for the newspapers had begun to report on Hitler's rise to power in Germany.

The snow began about midday and grew heavier by two o'clock. It would be dark soon. My knapsack had grown light. One more house before a long stretch of open field. I would quit after the next one. I moved steadily on my skis, breaking the new snow and enjoying the rhythm. The exercise helped to work off my anguish about things at home.

I caught a glimpse of the house in the swirling snow. Something about the white-painted farm home startled me. I knew that house. Could it be the *prest*'s house? My heart pounded. I could not summon the courage to face the *prest*.

"Fear of men will lead you astray." That line of Scripture came to me and urged me on. I prayed for help. Slowly I approached the house and removed my skis. My clothes were covered with snow, so I brushed myself and used the broom by the door to sweep off my lower legs and boots. I knocked.

A handsome silver-haired man answered. "Ragna!" he cried immediately. "Come in."

To my relief, it was not the *prest*. The elderly man was Herr Britt, my first grade religion teacher. "I'd better explain what I am doing before I accept your invitation to come in," I said. But I noticed he was a frail-looking man, so I swallowed my explanation and stepped in to close the door against the wind. His wife addressed me politely, much too politely, but he soon dispatched her to the kitchen to make coffee.

We sat down and talked. He listened intently. It was warm inside this man's home. I relaxed. When I finished talking, he looked at me and said, "Ragna, if you have found something you can really believe in, then hang on to it!"

I left that home fortified and ready to tackle the world. I felt I had passed some kind of test. I skied back to Steinkjer through heavy new snow, now lying in folds and dimples, like plump marshmallow sculpture in the protected places.

Chapter

Bumps and Bruises

"What is this crazy religion of yours?" my sister demanded when I arrived home. My two married sisters stood behind her in the main room. My brother waved a local newspaper.

"See here, the *prest* has written an article exposing your International Bible Students. He says it is a heresy spawned in America, a false religion. How deeply are you involved in this?"

"Let me explain. It is not false, it is from the Bible. The Bible says. . ."

"The *prest*, who knows a lot more than you, says it is straight from the devil."

"He should know the truth."

"Are you trying to bring shame on the whole family?"

"Have you lost your mind?"

"The whole town is talking about you."

They refused to let me explain. I left them and went to my room. I sat down and wrote an answer to that *prest*. I gave a full summary of the truth of what the brotherhood believes. I signed my pen name, Ragna Agnes Opdahl, and wrote underneath it, "International Bible Student."

Next morning I handed my rebuttal to the newspaper editor. He was more than willing to print it. I believed my article would silence the buzzing townfolk but more importantly educate my own family to the true facts.

How wrong I was! When the newspaper came out, not only my brothers and sisters but my gentle father flew into an uproar.

How could you have the nerve to answer a clergyman?" *Far* demanded, smacking the newspaper against his open palm. "How can I show my face in church again? You have disgraced the family."

Far did go to church, probably to pray for my salvation, and the *prest* asked him to remain after the service. He spoke seriously to *Far*, warning him against my dangerous religion. My father must take steps to save my soul. *Far* came home determined to change my mind. He talked past *middag* and let the food be ruined. He talked until he ran out of arguments. He could not sway me. For each accusation, I took my answer from the Bible. At last he threw up his hands. "What more can I say to convince you?"

"Nothing," I replied. "*Far*, I love you but I cannot give this up."

There was a long silence. The light in the room had grown dim but I could see that *Far* had tears in his eyes. Finally he said, "Ragna, I think you had better go back to Oslo."

"What do you mean, *Far*?"

"I am asking you to leave, Ragna. You cannot stay here any more."

I felt like *Far* had hit me. A great lump rose in my throat. I looked at him and realized that we were worlds apart, that my own father was a stranger who did not understand me. I jumped and ran upstairs. I began throwing things into my cheap brown suitcase. What would become of me? Alfredo was gone, *Mor* was gone, Freda belonged more to *Tante* Margit than to me. No one waited for me in Oslo. I caught sight of my dispirited face in the looking glass. I studied myself, wallowing in self-pity for a moment. Then I scolded the mirror, "This won't do." The Bible says we should rejoice in the time of trial. I took some cold water from the pitcher on the chest beneath the mirror and splashed my face in the bowl. I would cry about my family's rejection later. Right now, I needed to think about getting back to Oslo.

Back in the capital, I threw myself into my work. About forty-eight of us worked out of the city's tiny headquarters. I, being alone and free to travel, worked more and more in the country. I rode the train and took my bicycle or skis to cover the rural districts. A sweet British sister, a former ballerina, gave me her English bicycle when she returned to Britain due to health problems. I quickly ruined her fine bicycle on the rough Norwegian roads. The brakes had nearly seen their last when I crossed a hilltop one day and began to coast down a long, steep hill. The failing brakes had given me some wild rides that week but nothing like what lay in store. I looked

Double Trouble

ahead as I gained momentum and saw a metal gate at the bottom of the hill, placed there to confine the cows. I pumped the brakes but they barely slowed me. The bike flew as I neared the gate. "Jehovah, help me!" I jumped over the bike. I heard a sickening crash when the bike hit the gate. I lay there, not moving. It struck me that I was not dead. Everything hurt, mostly my arm, but nothing pained enough to be broken. I tried moving just a little. Then I heard a snort--a familiar sound. I looked up. Not one, but two bulls stood glaring at me from across the road amid the pine trees. Springing to my feet with superhuman energy, I gathered my spilled books and possessions in a single move and bolted down the hill. I threw my book bag over the gate with one hand and vaulted the bicycle over with the other. My body followed. Just in time. The two bulls charged after me. From the safety of the gate, I could see they were young bulls. Nevertheless they had the right attitude.

I surveyed my cuts and bruises, brushing the road dust and tiny rocks from my scrapes. The bicycle lay in shambles. I faced a two mile walk to the next village. I limped along, pushing my ruined bike and lugging the books on my sore shoulder. Before long, I spied a horse and wagon some distance away on a side road. Thank heaven! I sat down to wait. As it approached, I saw that the horse pulled not a farm wagon but a funeral wagon. A kind elderly driver offered me a ride. I climbed on, casting a nervous glance at the hearse behind me. "Oh, no," the man laughed. "I have already delivered the body. I am on my way home from the funeral." He took me to a place where I had my bicycle repaired--enough to last till my return to Oslo.

Back in the city, a helpful brother found me a good second-hand bike. I was ready to go again. The movement had introduced a new tool for evangelization, a small portable gramophone with music, Bible records and teaching. It bothered me that though the reader had a good distinct voice, he had to clear his throat many times during the message--but people didn't notice. I visited my first farmhouse with the phonograph and asked the householder if I could have five minutes of time with him and his family. "Yes, yes, of course," the farmer answered. He collected his wife, some aunts and uncles, grandparents and several young children around a large dining table. While they gathered, he accepted one of my books and subscribed to the *Watchtower* magazine. Oh, this is not so difficult at all, I gloated to myself as I turned on the gramophone. Everyone sat motionless while I played the music. They remained just as silent when I started the Bible teaching records. Then, one by one, the members of the family disappeared. When the last one got up and left, I sat alone with the gramophone blaring into an empty room. I let the record finish, then I closed the machine. "Thank you," I called in a loud voice. I let myself out of the house.

My bewilderment was mixed with hunger pangs. Normally, the hospitable farm folk offered me coffee and waffles or breakfast cake as a *formiddag* snack. My stomach told me the meal hour had long passed and the next farmhouse lay a good stiff pedal away. But then I was always hungry. The country air and the good exercise stimulated my appetite.

I remember the aroma of freshly-boiled coffee wafting from the kitchen of one prosperous-looking farm home as I leaned my bicycle against a birch tree. A young fresh-faced girl opened the door. Behind her lay stacks of sandwiches on a tray, fragrant cakes and homemade cookies. How wonderful! Then I remembered my manners. "You must be having a party," I smiled. "I will come back later. Why don't you take a moment to read this witness card. Then you'll know what to expect when I come back."

The servant girl read my card and asked if she could bring it in to the guests. I waited many minutes. When she returned, she invited me to join the party. I protested, "Oh, no. I don't wish to intrude." "*Kom*," she laughed and led me to a large wood-paneled room where twenty or more people lined a table laden with sandwiches, dried fish, cheeses, *smorbrod*, fruit preserves and coffee. I apologized. "I don't wish to disturb your party." My eyes feasted on the delicious things to eat.

"It's not a party. We're having a religious meeting," a stern man at the head of the table retorted. "Since you too believe in the Almighty, we have decided to hear your message."

They passed me platters of good foods and I ate while they looked at my *Watchtower* magazines. The man next to me riffled the pages, then suddenly stopped. He put his finger on President Rutherford's name and passed the magazine to a lady next to him. She stared and pointed out the American leader's name to someone else. Conversation quieted. I gulped down the last of my sandwich.

"What do you think of our president?" I asked with a hopeful smile.

Silence. They all looked at one another. I felt a strong desire to disappear.

Finally: "Poor, poor girl! An old lady shook a bony finger at me. "What have you gotten yourself into?"

I looked at her with raised eyebrows.

"Rutherford is an American false prophet," a straight-backed elderly man intoned. "He does not believe in hellfire."

"Is that so awful?" I submitted.

"Oh, *ja, ja!* It is heresy. And if you do not stop going around with such a teaching, you will burn in hell with your Mr. Rutherford."

I allowed myself a remark: "Are you quite sure you won't be there to welcome us?"

"*Ja*, we are saved in Jesus' blood."

"Friends, we must pray for this young woman," the leader insisted. He looked at me over his spectacles. "We will pray that you will be saved."

"That prayer won't go farther than the ceiling," I said, rising to my feet.

They stared.

"Thank you for the coffee. And good-bye!"

While I ran into an occasional stone wall like these sour sectarians, my pioneer service yielded wonderful results overall. My brothers and sisters at the Bethel Home headquarters in Oslo stood amazed at my total 2,000 subscriptions placed to *Watchtower* during my first seven years pioneering in the bone-poor days of the middle 1930s. Our name had changed from International Bible Students to Jehovah's Witnesses in 1931, about the time I joined. I witnessed to thousands, bringing the Truth in spoken word and printed tract to countless Norwegian families.

Freda blossomed into a healthy, active and talented little miss under *Tante* Margit's loving supervision. She started skiing at age three. When she reached school age, she began ski racing. I loved to watch. She played the piano and did well in school. My pioneer service did not prevent me from enjoying her childhood parties. (Why don't you have a new dress, Mother?" she always asked me.) When I left for the country, I said, "I will be back to see you when the *Hvitveis* bloom" or "When the snow comes, so will I."

I felt a twinge of guilt leaving Freda, even though she looked perfectly happy. *Tante* Margit had opened her home to two little boys, sons of a widower sea captain. They became Freda's brothers and the house rang with their boisterous play. If I had worried about her becoming prissy, I could now take comfort in her tomboy activities. She had everything yet I always felt an invisible cord tugging me back when I said goodbye.

I suppose I indulged myself with fantasies of staying in Oslo to raise Freda myself when I began to dread preparing alone for each

Tante Margit, her niece Astrid, and three-year old Freda prepare for a spring ski outing.

upcoming trip. The books we started using came packed in large, heavy cartons--no more pamphlets in a light backpack. Lugging those unwieldy cartons along with my bicycle and belongings exhausted me. The young man who supplied my books at the Bethel Home, Erling Dahl, always hurried around the counter to carry my boxes outside for me. I began to find notes from him tucked in with my books. "Have a nice trip. See you when you get back." Sometimes he hid a little candy in my box, or when shortages made that unavailable, a bit of dried fruit.

How I wished for a helper the day I took the bus to Rena. The driver did his best, despite an overcrowded bus and a pouring rainstorm. Somehow we loaded on my three cartons and the ever-present bicycle. The rain came down in sheets, so much that the driver had to pull off the road. When we started up again, I asked him if he could recommend a place to stay near Rena. He promised to call me when we arrived at the *Pensionat* he suggested.

The rain continued to stream down when he stopped at a boardinghouse. I understood he could not drench himself carrying my heavy boxes to the door. He knew I had books and gave me a large rag to protect the cartons. I took off my raincoat to cover the remaining boxes and got them to the porch. "My, my, who would be out in this weather?" a woman exclaimed, opening the door. "Come in, come in. Let me help you."

What a relief to be inside! Water flowed out of my shoes, making small puddles on her polished wooden floor. I smiled at my hostess.

"I am a Jehovah's Witness. I have come to do pioneer work in your district. I'd like a room for a week or two."

Her face clouded. "Oh, I see. You are one of them."

"Yes," I smiled weakly. "I am... one of them."

"Well," she drew in a sharp breath, "we have only one room to offer you. It's out back, over the old stable."

I looked outside at the downpour. "I don't mind as long as it is clean."

"The cost is 25 *kroner* per week, plus extra for fresh sheets," she snapped.

I sighed. "*Ja*, I'll take it."

A maid followed me with the sheets as I lugged my boxes through the rain out back to the deserted stable. She helped carry the cartons up a narrow stairway. The room had two beds. The maid removed the sheets from the bed I chose and said, "The *husfrue* says you must put on the sheets yourself." As she started downstairs I said, "Wait a moment. What is that door?"

"Two manfolk sleep there."

"Two manfolk!" Do they have to go through here to get to their room?"

She laughed. "*Ja, ja*. But they will not hurt you. Good night."

I made the bed and collapsed onto it. Happily, the coffee in my thermos had stayed warm. It and the sandwiches I had packed cheered me up. A clothes hook beside each of the two doors gave me an idea. I removed the rope from one of my book cartons. Then I knotted the rope on one hook and strung it across to the other. Perfect! I removed the used sheets from the other bed and hung them up. The jerry-rigged curtain shielded my bed from view. I undressed to my skimpy gown and climbed into bed with a book. Not long after, I heard heavy boots clumping up the stairway. The door swung open, hit the rope and knocked down my drapery. A man, about 60 years old, gasped in surprise, staring at the blond lady in bed.

"Oh, excuse me," he fumbled, picking up the sheets. "I'll help you hang these up again."

"No, no, thank you," I replied in a terse voice. "Just go on to your room."

"I'll tell my roommate you're here," the workman said. "I'll listen for him and let him know."

"Thank you very kindly." I pretended to read my book. He clumped into the next room.

During the night, the rain began to leak through the eaves. I spent most of my sleeping time rearranging my book cartons to keep them dry. I was fully dressed by dawn. I tried to read until a knock came from the other side of the door.

My embarrassed but kind-looking "neighbor" stood in the doorway. "Please don't be afraid. My friend and I would like to help you."

He carried my books downstairs. He offered the address of a better boardinghouse in town. "You must be an International Bible Student--I ran into your group during my years in America." He had read Rutherford's books. I gave him the newest book and we talked while I waited for the next bus to town. He helped me onto the bus and waved goodbye. While we bounced along the dirt road, I thanked Jehovah for always sending me an angel when I needed one.

Erling never met Mor, but I showed him this mid-1920s picture with my parents, three of my six sisters, Jens and Jakob (far right). I stand behind my nephew, Jakob Weideman, now a famous European painter.

Chapter

My Special Angel

Jehovah kept another angel for me stationed full-time at the Bethel Home in the person of Erling Dahl. He's nine years younger than me, and a man, I mused, but he's becoming my best friend. We often talked for hours as he lingered over assembling and packing my books. Erling had an openness to people. He also had a special way with women though he was certainly "a man's man"--athletic, especially in track and field and skiing. His father, before his death, served as the postmaster general of Skotfoss in Telemark. Erling ran or skied with the mail pouch from childhood. I decided he was almost handsome, lean and strong with well-chiseled features. He would make some girl a nice husband. What amused me about Erling was his hands. They were too big for him. They didn't seem to know where to rest. When he talked, his hands got in the way. But they were capable hands, amazingly strong and deft at work.

We talked about many things, mostly our religion. His family, too, hated Jehovah's Witness beliefs. Erling grew up with endless religious meetings and church services. He left that behind, as I did, when he found the Truth.

Erling read constantly. He watched the Germans build their war machine through the newspapers. We talked about the Nazis during the winter of 1939. Germany invaded Poland that year. It sent a chill of foreboding through us. Things looked ominous for our Scandinavian neighbor, Finland, Erling said. We wondered about Hitler, the Anti-Christ and Armageddon, which the Bible prophesies.

Erling would switch the conversation from the Nazis back to

light-hearted banter within the blink of an eye. He loved to joke and make fun.

I hadn't seen Erling for over a month one spring morning when I visited the Bethel Home for a book order to take on my next assignment. He was in a merry mood as he gathered my materials.

"I'm watching you pack my books." I smiled at him across the counter.

"May I ask why?" His brown eyes twinkled.

"I want to see what little surprise you will slip in. Thank you for the dried apples in with my *Enemies* books. They were delicious. I wondered how many ration coupons you used. Tell me, do you treat all the lady pioneers so kindly?"

For once, Erling did not return a quick answer. He paused and glanced about the building for signs of his superior. "No, Ragna," he said in a quiet voice. "Just for you."

"Well!" I said, somewhat stupidly. I felt myself reddening like a schoolgirl. "Why me?"

"Because you are special. I like you very much. Sometimes I'm tempted to walk away from my job and go off traveling with you. If you would let me, that is."

"Me, travel with you? Certainly not!"

I hadn't meant to be so harsh. I could see that I had embarrassed him. I softened.

"I mean, it would not be proper. Besides, you would be crazy to give up your job here. You would lose your nice, free room. With the Germans blowing up cities all over Europe, many young brothers would want your safe job and room here in Oslo. Take my advice, you don't want to be a fox without a nest, like me."

I took the mother role to put him off. I was confused by the notion that this young man had romance on his mind. But... there was an undeniable electricity in the air.

"Oh, my, it's late!", I exclaimed. "I have an errand. I'll come back later for the books."

Erling hurried around the counter and placed his tall, angular frame in front of me. "I hope I haven't offended you." He reached out and grasped my forearms. "Please let me talk with you. I can close the book department for a while and take a *middag* break. Please... we'll walk to the park."

I felt a growing sense of amazement at this man. What in the world did he plan to say? I mentally postponed my plans for leaving Oslo on the 4 p.m. train. Erling seemed so earnest. I could leave tomorrow instead.

We strode the tree-lined Karl Johan Boulevard toward Frogner Park. Erling transferred his mental energy to his long legs and I pushed to keep up. Since he looked distressed, I talked. We passed the playful Vigeland statues in the park. "My brother, Kristoffer, knows Gustav Vigeland, the sculptor," I chattered. "Some people wanted Vigeland to do Norwegian heroes and saints, like St. Olaf, but he filled the park with statues of children and families. Kristoffer said Vigeland received criticism--a lot at first--but now people seem to like his work."

After a while I ran out of things to say. I think the talking calmed me down more than Erling. A soft spring breeze brushed my face and arms. It seemed especially pleasant because winter's stinging wind remained so fresh in my memory.

"Let's sit here," Erling said abruptly.

He sat and didn't say a word. Sensing the energy inside him, I feared he would burst. Finally he said, "I've been thinking a lot lately, Ragna."

"About what?"

"When I suggested traveling with you, I didn't mean... well, I was serious. I'd like to go about witnessing with you. I don't care about my job at the headquarters anymore. Henrik can have it. What I'd really like to do... what I have thought about doing... is to leave here and come help you. I want very much to do that." He looked into my eyes now and I looked right inside him. There was a strength I liked. When he stopped joking, a whole new person emerged from behind the merry face. I looked away.

"I don't know what to say, Erling. There's one thing that isn't clear. Do you want to marry me?"

Relief crossed his well-boned face. "Why not?" he demanded, grinning.

"Well, for one thing, I am older than you!" I retorted. "And I won't give up my witnessing to keep house for a man. To be plain, I've decided never to remarry. I want nothing to interfere with my pioneer service."

"I don't want you to stop your pioneering. I want to help you with it. We can be a team. Ride our bicycles together, camp at night, share everything. We won't have much but I believe Jehovah will watch over us."

"Erling, there are lots of sweet girls who would make a happy home for you. Why do you want to marry *me?*"

"I've been thinking about that too. There's no one like you, Ragna. So alive, so determined, so dedicated. I love that. I decided I would have to speak now or you would slip out of my life. Will you marry me, Ragna?"

He looked so serious and so kind. I needed his support. I had for a long time needed a friend, a helper. I thought of Alfredo, my love, my husband... a different man from a different world, far removed from Oslo, from today. I sat there a long time, absorbed deep inside myself, experiencing feelings from the past. Reidar's betrayal... Alfredo's death... I didn't want that pain again. Everything in my emotions cried, "No." But something deeper in my spirit said, "Yes." It rose up quiet, sure and strong, saying "Yes!" I felt a rush of happiness spring up, coming from deep down and flowing out to fill my consciousness.

"Yes." I repeated what I heard inside me.

"Do you mean it?"

"Yes!"

We took each other's hands and smiled into each other's eyes. I realized that I had never really touched Erling. His big warm hands felt good. The park was full of mothers and children. We didn't embrace. We just smiled into one another's eyes.

. . .

"How does July 15 sound to you?" Erling inquired happily over the telephone the next day. "I'm coming to take you to the depot and help with shipping your bicycle. You can tell me then. We really need to set the date right away. You'll be gone the next two weeks. I want to have definite plans for us to talk about when you come back."

At the Oslo station I waved goodbye. I leaned back in the worn passenger seat and smiled. I had someone to come home to. I felt happy about our new life together... friends, husband and wife, a team. Sunlight poured in the window and bathed my body in its warmth.

Two weeks of pioneering at farm homes flew by. I returned to Oslo with enough time to select a pale blue gabardine suit, tailored with the flawless fit fashionable in Europe just then. I was glad to be trim at age thirty-nine, in better shape than at twenty because of my constant exercise. I selected a matching blue hat, wonderful with my eyes, and a pair of white pumps. I remembered my Confirmation shoes, so precious twenty-five years ago. I felt young again, embarking on a new life. A shadow passed through my mind--World War I had spoiled my passage into adulthood. War clouds loomed over Europe again today...

We had to settle for a civil ceremony because Norwegian law prohibited a Jehovah's Witness from performing a marriage ceremony. Erling took me to the Oslo town hall, where his two cousins waited. We shook hands, then we all trooped upstairs to the Justice of the Peace. In no time at all, Erling and I became man and wife.

The cousins smiled and shook hands, said "Congratulations" and shook hands again. I felt strange, to be married, yet not in a church. What would *Mor* say? Yet, these were different days. Erling hurried me off. We planned to travel to Scotfoss, his home town, to meet his mother.

"My family thinks I'm crazy," he laughed. "Now I've *married* a Witness! They're all in shock. I want them to meet you and see what a lovely lady you are. They're expecting a religious fanatic, you know."

Snapped by street photographer enroute to our wedding, Erling and I embark on a new life.

"It can't be any worse than what my family will say. They don't know what I'll do next--but they're sure they're not going to like it."

The next weeks passed in a happy blur. A party at Erling's mother's home... her warm welcome... a houseful of young brothers and sisters... a crystal bowl heaped with ruby red cherries and a comic wedding verse hidden among the fruits... honeymoon on a borrowed boat... bicycling together on sun-splashed mountain mornings... waking up secure in Erling's arms.

We returned to a little room we had rented in Oslo before the wedding. We began pioneering together. Sometimes Erling went down to the quay on the Oslofjord and witnessed to the fishermen on their boats there. In the morning, they would offer him a glass of cod liver oil and swallow their portion with a hearty "*Skaal!*" Despite increasingly severe food shortages, the Norwegians remained generous. Erling always managed to surprise me with a bit of ham one day, some eggs and sugar the next. I packed a picnic to enjoy in the summer forest as we bicycled from door to door. In farm districts I never worried about where to sleep. Erling always found a place. One night in late summer, a kind farmer offered his hayloft for the night. I took a swim in a nearby river to freshen up while Erling picked the sweet yellow cloudberries that grew wild along the water. We feasted on the delicious berries, covered with some sweet cream Erling bought, so thick it would scarcely pour from the bottle. I kissed Erling goodnight and settled down in the fragrant hay. The fresh air, the vigorous bicycle trip, the long day made me luxuriously sleepy. I dozed in moments and the long, light evening turned to moonless black.

I woke up screaming.

"Something bit me! A rat! Oh, Erling!"

Something rustled away in the darkness.

I spent the whole night waiting for the rat to return. Erling's comforting words had little effect. When the farmer's wife rattled the milk cans at 5 a.m. I hurried down the loft ladder to ask for some disinfectant.

"Ooo! *Ja, ja,* it was the mink. Ooo. What a bite!"

"The mink? Surely it was a rat, *ja?*"

"No, no. Come to the kitchen with me. I will get some onion. The mink farm is across the potato field and sometimes the animals come to the barn. That's a mink bite. I know by the deep cut. You must have had a fright."

The good wife laid a large slice of onion over my wound. It felt better. I thanked the woman and left with Erling. The onion worked magic to heal the mink's deep bite. But I couldn't put an onion slice on my imagination.

"That's the last time I'll sleep in a hayloft," I told Erling.

. . .

The wildflowers disappeared. Soon the mountain meadows turned to rust and gold. Winter came. Erling and I strapped our feet onto skis for our daily travels. We were so happy. We often returned to Oslo to visit Freda. I watched as Erling played with Freda, listened to her delighted laughter. I felt complete. Not only had I found a deep loving friendship with my young husband, but Freda had gained a fond stepfather. The world couldn't be a better place. Winter wore on. Its meager light yielded to March's early-dawning days. We looked forward to celebrating our first anniversary, the culmination of a precious first year together.

"Shall we go to Lillehammer for the spring vacation?" Erling asked me one day. "The hotels will be packed with skiers during Easter week. We can distribute our books to many who might not otherwise hear the message. We can take a little time to ski--probably for the last time this season."

I knew Lillehammer well. A charming ski resort town with a historical park, Lillehammer attracted many vacationers from Oslo. I remembered a farmhouse there where I had rented a cozy little room over the barn. It would be fun to go back there with Erling.

"What a good idea," I replied. "Everyone in Oslo is glum. All this talk of war--Hitler and the invasion of Poland and Nazis and bombs--it's all I hear. In Lillehammer people will be happy--like us."

I hugged Erling, pretending to be gay, but the talk of war did bother me. Norway had declared itself neutral, along with Sweden and Denmark, but Norway's neutrality had already begun to crumble. Norwegian ships assisted the British. Several British and German naval skirmishes had occurred in Norwegian waters with little official protest from Oslo. How long before the British or French would mine our territorial waters and blow up a German supply ship? People feared reprisal. Some Norwegians expected an ultimatum from Germany. Others believed that Norway could stay out of the conflict. At Lillehammer, the spring sunshine would drive away thoughts of war. People would ski in sweaters and shorts. There would be picnics in the snow and jokes, the laughter of children free from school.

"Our work may not pay much but it does give us our freedom," Erling winked. "Let's go."

Erling resembled Jens, shown here. My new husband became my brother, my friend, my spouse, replacing the family I lost when I became a Witness.

Chapter

Trapped in Lillehammer

Hitler's war darkened 1940 Europe, but we didn't really feel it. In Norway spring sunshine softened winter's brittle grip and drove away the shadow of global conflict. How could we be unhappy on a sunny April afternoon? We were pedaling our bicycles along a puddle-pocked street in Lillehammer. A pencil-pointed church steeple stabbed at the blue sky. Patches of open water on mountain-rimmed Lake Mjosa reflected the blue. We had just visited an outdoor museum displaying Norway's farm and folk life. Called *Maihaugen*, the historic village had a gallery that housed bright painted Norwegian sleighs from the era of Eric Bloodaxe and tapestries that depicted ancient kings quaffing mead at a banquet table.

"*Maihaugen* reminded me of my childhood," I said as we cruised along. "*Tante* Cecilia's place looked like the first farm group we saw there."

"*Ja*, I'm glad they have preserved those old buildings. They were built to last. We need to remember the Norway of the past. There is much simple beauty in the hand-carved furniture."

Lillehammer's historic park struck a chord in my consciousness. Here in Norway, my people had lived, worked and died since before the Vikings. The rugged northland produced a strong, vigorous people, who conquered the challenge of the sea and tamed the mountainous land. Things were changing now. I felt a yearning for the security of my childhood, those simple, safe early years.

Erling broke my reverie. "Let's test these new bicycles. I'll race you to the cafe."

We cut through Lillehammer's winding streets laughing. Sidewalks overflowed with skiers and tourists, a parade of multi-colored ski sweaters and knicker socks. Our sturdy new bikes were not designed for racing. Like *Far*'s well-muscled workhorses, they carried their load, but failed to fly like the sleek stallions he loved to race.

We braked, breathless from the workout and laughing, outside a little cafe at nearly two o'clock. *Herr* Bjornson, the restaurant owner, and his wife greeted us, smiling. During our three weeks, Erling and I had often come to this friendly place, for the food cost little and tasted good. We had placed one of our books with the wife. "Have you heard the news?" *Fru* Bjornson asked. "The radio said that a German ship blew up in the Oslofjord yesterday. Hundreds of Germans were killed."

"What kind of ship? A commercial ship?" Erling frowned.

"Oh, we don't know. Such a shame. So many drowned, they say. We've been trying to hear more, but our radio is dead."

Erling looked at me for a moment. Then he ordered our soup. A few minutes later, *Fru* Bjornson served the steaming bowls, chuckling, "It's a good thing you didn't want the Mjosa salmon. *Herr* Bjornson cannot cook. The power has failed. But I don't worry. We keep the soup hot on the woodstove and we can offer cold cuts till we run out, if the power does not come on again. You know life in these mountains. Heavy spring snows knock down our power lines." All the time she spoke she nodded vigorously, her gray-blond curls bouncing and plump jowls bobbing.

"But there is no storm," Erling protested. "It hasn't snowed all week."

"Ah, then, we must ask *Herr* Nygard across the street. He always knows what is happening."

Fru Bjornson bustled out and soon returned with a portly bewhiskered man in a fish-seller's apron, gesturing and talking loudly. "Harald! Listen to what *Herr* Nygard has to say," she cried.

"It's the Germans--German soldiers in Oslo, God help us." *Herr* Nygard rolled his eyes heavenward.

"My brother has just received a message from our cousin in Hamar. He's got a wireless radio. The ship that exploded in the Oslofjord--it was a German battleship on its way to attack Oslo."

A murmur went up from the group. "No, this cannot be true," someone said.

"It *is* true," the fish-seller insisted. "All the radio stations and the telegraph have been seized. My brother says German planes bombed the harbor at Oslo to get their ships through, then they bombed the city and landed 15,000 troops. The King has fled Oslo." *Herr* Nygard gulped for air, flushed of face and breathing too hard for an overweight man of his age.

A small crowd had gathered to see what caused the disturbance.

"The Germans have landed everywhere--not only at Oslo, but Christiansand, Stavanger, Bergen, Trondheim and even as far north as Narvik, they say. Johan, my brother, has gone to the town hall to spread the news. He heard the railroad has shut down because Norwegians have blown up bridges to stop the German advance."

"Invasion! But this can't be!" cried Erling.

"What about Freda? And *Tante* Margit? They are right there, near Oslo, where they are bombing," I said.

"A rider just arrived on horseback from Elverum," a young man rushed up to say. "The King is safe. He escaped to Hamar, but the Germans chased him and he's now in hiding at Elverum."

Elverum! Just the next valley east of Lillehammer. Erling and I exchanged a long look. "How can the world turn upside down--in a day?" I demanded. "War! It's stupid! Why war? Why now?"

The street buzzed with people passing the news from group to group, from shop to shop. People gathered in excited clumps, everyone shouting questions. Slowly the congregation of strangers melded into one people, strangers comforting strangers, sharing a common sense of shock and grief.

"My mother is at home in Oslo," a lady sobbed.

"Our children are staying in the city with their grandparents," a man said. "There's no way to find out if they are all right."

A middle-aged woman kept trying to dial the dead telephone and shouting, "Operator? Operator! I must make a call." People tried to console her, but she kept on dialing, like a dreamer in a nightmare struggling in vain to thwart disaster. Men returned from the railway station. "There's a mob of people demanding to go to Oslo," a young father with his children clustered close reported. "But there are no trains. There are no trains to anywhere."

Erling and I returned to our little room to find the *husmor* changing the sheets. "You must go back to Oslo," she said. "I have the *prest* from Hamar coming here. We must give this room to the man of God. And you remember your time was up last week."

She was right. When the rental period expired we had asked for a few more days.

"We have nowhere to go in Lillehammer," Erling explained. "The railroad has shut down. We cannot return to Oslo."

"You can sleep in the stable till the train starts running again," the landlady said, shaking her head. "War... everything changed overnight." Her eyes filled with tears. "Here, take one of my blankets. I am sorry I cannot help you more."

After a miserable night huddled under a single blanket on the cold stable floor, Erling and I took stock of our situation.

"Every hotel in town is packed. The town will soon run low on food. We're without a room, we have very little money, and there's no way to leave Lillehammer," Erling said.

"We're trapped," I agreed. "But at least we're trapped together, Erling. I am so glad I am not alone, like I was before."

"I am glad we are together, too, my dear. But we must concentrate on staying warm and safe--as well as together."

He began to pace the barn floor.

"Why Norway?" Erling shook his fist. "Why now? I can't understand the Germans. Well, the British will be into this in no time. Norwegians will fight, but we must have Britain's air support to succeed. If only you and I had a place to stay. We won't need a place for long--the Allies will make quick work of driving the Germans from our ports."

"How about Steinkjer?"

"Steinkjer! But that's more than 300 miles from here, Ragna. And with the bridges destroyed, the only route would take us across the mountains. No, Steinkjer is out."

He scanned my face, shaking his head. "I know you'd like to go home, Ragna. But Steinkjer--there is no way. If we could ride the bicycles, maybe. But with roads closed, it's impossible."

I waited. He paced back and forth.

"Oh, maybe you're right. Steinkjer may not be a bad idea. This tourist town will face empty cupboards in less than a week, and Steinkjer has the farms and fjord--the little towns will live on potatoes and fish till this thing is over."

He stopped pacing to look at me again.

"We can't stay here, you know. Where could we find a place anywhere in central Norway?--except Steinkjer. Your father still has his big home. Steinkjer is away from everything the Germans want. A safe place, if there is such a thing with Germans crawling all over our shoreline. It won't be easy, Ragna. First we'll have to cross the mountain range from Lillehammer to Rena. That's about 35 miles. You know, there's a serious chance we might not make it." He regarded me darkly. "There are spring blizzards in these mountains. What if we got lost? And crossing a mountain range in April means traveling in slush. Can we make it slogging through 35 miles of that?"

"We can travel at night, when the crust forms," I replied. "We can do it, Erling. It's our only choice."

He sighed. "Jehovah will help us, Ragna. Let us pray together."

We knelt in the drafty stable. The milk cows gazed mildly on, while Erling prayed to God for guidance on the dangerous journey. He prayed for help and protection. He prayed for strength.

Then he sprang to his feet, full of energy and decision. "Come Ragna, we'll rent some extra skis and build a sled. The man at the ski shop has his walls papered with maps. When I spoke to him last week, he mentioned hunting and fishing in these mountains since he was a boy. Perhaps he'll help us find a route."

Arne Bojer called his oldest son to help study the maps with Erling. Hikers and hardy ski travelers used the mountain trail to Rena. (It later became the route of a famous ski race, the Birkebeiner.) While the men traced ridges and stream drainages on the well-used maps, I spoke with Sigrid Bojer, a kind woman, slim and athletic like her husband.

"Oh, you cannot travel in your dress," *Fru* Bojer exclaimed. "Where are your ski pants?"

"I have none," I answered. "Can you trade me a pair? I'll give you my dress."

"Heavens, my only extra pants are worn--and awfully baggy. But I'll show them to you."

I looked ruefully at my nice winter dress, then removed it and put on Sigrid's old pants with her woolen sweater. "It's a deal," I smiled. "Thank you, I really do need these pants."

Erling worked furiously to construct a sled.

"We'll use the sled to carry our bicycles, Ragna. I'm glad we spent the extra money on the heavy-duty model--they may save our lives. I want to finish this sled by noon. Then we'll rest and be ready to leave tonight."

He built an ingenious sled, a wooden platform with skis attached to the bottom. He designed the sled to carry the stout bicycles, along with food for the journey, and the barest minimum of supplies--our ski wax, the blankets, sun lotion, and a single change of clothes. Everything else--books, clothing, toiletries--we would leave behind.

As Erling rigged the sled with rope and Arne Bojer applied klister wax to our skis, a young man approached.

"Do you remember me? I am Jakob, the one you spoke to last week at the hotel."

I remembered the man. He had been in a group at the Hotel

Mjosa. The men had carried on a heated discussion of Vidkun Quisling, the Oslo pro-Nazi politician.

"You must take me with you. I hear you are going to Steinkjer. I must get across the range to Osterdalen. Please, let me join you."

Erling eyed Jakob's overweight knapsack. It spoke of a man who knew little of the mountains.

"And your skis?" Erling asked.

"I don't ski. But I am a good walker. My legs are very strong. I will keep up with you, you will soon see that."

Erling withdrew to the ski shop and I followed. "We cannot say no," he whispered. "We have met him before. It would not be right to turn away a man, friend or stranger, in this time of war."

I agreed. Erling glanced reluctantly through the window at the nervous young man. "God be with us," he said looking into my eyes. "Let us go."

We trudged through muddy Lillehammer, Erling dragging the sled along stretches of still frozen snow. Ice formed along the edges of the spring puddles, a good sign. We prayed for a cold night and frozen snow to speed our journey. Jakob walked behind to help Erling when the sled stuck. I carried the skis. We reached the town's edge. Lights glowed warm from small windows in the white-painted homes there. I looked ahead at the dark mountainside and shivered. I leaned over to wind my ski binding strap around my clumsy rubber boot, the only boots I had, and tried to secure the strap. Suddenly, I did not want to go into those dark, icy mountains. I just wanted to go home. I wondered if I had a home anymore.

Chapter

Ordeal on Skis

"*Herr* Dahl! Is that you?" a voice called in the dim lingering light. "*Ja,* who is it?" answered Erling peering across the field at two figures hurrying along the road.

"Petter Bojer, Arne's son. My friend here will travel with you."

The pair crossed the field. I recognized Petter. The boy with him strode lightly across the snow, tall, blond and vigorous.

"This is Erik. He's from a village in the mountains. He is a strong skier and he, too, needs to cross the range."

Erik smiled and I liked him immediately. He reminded me of Jens, hardy, capable and confident. Erling said "*Velkommen*" and flashed me a pleased look.

We began gliding across the snow, with Jakob hurrying behind. We slowed to climb a trail that wound uphill along the mountain's forested flank. Conversation died as we concentrated on scaling the steep terrain.

The rich, broad Gudbrandsdal valley lay spread out below us, its fertile farms awaiting summer's plush green. We climbed higher and were rewarded for our work with a view of the soaring Jotunheimen, northern Europe's highest mountain range, behind us to the southwest.

Several hours later, we crossed an open saddle. The hard snow surface, causing a rhythmic scraping sound, let us skim along at a brisk pace. My spirits lifted. Jehovah was with us. He had sent a young mountaineer to guide us.

Erling's sled glided over the crust. Jakob marched behind. We stopped at midnight to share some coffee from a thermos bottle and eat some rye bread. To the north rose the Rondane, rounded peaks peaceful in the quiet dimness, a contrast to the staggering Jotunheimen across the valley.

I caught my second wind somewhere on the uphill trek and rode the crest of that energy through most of the night, but before the dawn, a cold wind blew. The temperature plummeted and the snow surface hardened to ice. Every step I took now caused my ski to slip backwards. I could no longer glide, but had to walk the slippery skis, one step at a time. Our group stopped to re-wax, but no wax gripped on the frustrating icy surface. Progress slowed. My spirits sank. Weariness crept into my body like a dark shadow. Erling began to cough. We stopped to rest, weary and downhearted.

"Look. The sky is beginning to brighten there in the east," Erik said. "Soon it will be light and in a few hours the sun will soften the snow. It's a clear night. It will be a beautiful morning."

Erik was right. Soon enough a crimson glow appeared on the saw-toothed Jotunheimen. I forgot my exhaustion to watch the sun's dazzling performance. A bank of clouds orchestrated color from vivid rose to lavender against the wild beauty of the range. Then the sun climbed the mountain staircase and burst into view. We continued along a ridgeline, climbing here and dropping there, silhouetted against the morning sky.

The sun warmed our backs as we crossed a large mountain bowl. Soon, Erik told us that we would begin the long descent to Rena. I let out a deep breath. Downhill! Erling's struggle would soon end. I watched his heaving back, worried. Then I moved ahead to speak to him. He looked so tired. "The worst is over," I said. "We're going to make it."

The sun grew hot. We stripped off hats, then coats and mittens and finally skied in shirt sleeves. The brilliant sun forced us to squint and seared our faces. We traversed the ridgeline until Erik stopped to point out a long, deeply cut valley disappearing into flat land far below. "That's our route," he cried. He swung his skis around to extend over the edge of a cornice and with a whoop dropped out of sight, like a man stepping off a cliff. Finally we spotted him below, laughing and waving. Erling chose a calmer descent, well beyond the cornice of wind-packed snow overhanging the ridge. He snowplowed to brake the push of the heavy sled behind him. Jakob slid and rolled, floundering down the steep slope, scraping his hands and bare arms on the abrasive ice-snow. I placed my feet on the edge of the cornice, so that the forward half of my skis extended out over nothing. I peered at Erik far below and wondered why he had slowed his pace to almost nothing. We had agreed to meet below at tree line where he planned to have a fire built and fresh coffee made.

I drew a breath and leaned forward. My heart slammed each beat. My ski tips angled downward. In an instant I plummeted from the ridge and shot diagonally through the wide, open mountain bowl. Cool air frosted my sunburned cheeks in an exhilarating rush as I swooped downward, finally braking my speed with telemark turns. The mountain's sheer wall plunged sharply, but after the initial dive my skis slowed on the soft snow. The lower I dropped, the slower I went. Shocked, I realized that the snow had turned to the consistency of mashed potatoes under the intense April sun.

Erik stood scraping caked snow from his skis, a layer almost two inches thick that adhered to the ski's bottom surface. "This doesn't look good," he confided. "Let's hope it's cooler down in the trees."

Noticing Erling, who strained to pull the heavy sled through the mush, Erik sprinted uphill to help. Then we waited for Jakob. He sank hip deep with every step as he labored to catch up.

When we resumed our travel, I felt a growing apprehension. We had to stop every few minutes to scrape the sticky snowpack from our skis. When we started out again, the skis immediately collected more snow, growing heavier with each step until they were impossible to drag along. I looked down the long valley at the many miles ahead. Fear flitted through my mind like a pesky fly.

The open bowl, brilliant in the sunshine, became a sinister place. I watched as Jakob waded, like a man walking through waist-deep mud, sinking and fighting for every step. He looked exhausted. He did not utter a word, but I noticed his lips moving. Our group moved into scrub trees, scattered here and there, just above timberline.

I heard a mild drone, coming from nowhere. The blue sky stretched above, uninterrupted by a single cloud. The sound intensified. Suddenly a plane burst over the ridge above and shot down toward us.

"A war plane. It's German," Erik cried. "Get down!" We threw ourselves onto the snow. The German plane circled the bowl and flew directly above our scattered party. I closed my eyes, trying to make myself invisible as the drone rose to a scream above me. I feared the plane would land on top of us.

Praise God for the handful of half-alive trees. They were runty and wind-scarred fir, but they disguised our presence, for the plane took another endless circle then headed down the valley toward the Osterdalen.

We hurried to cover in a conifer forest below timberline. When we reached the trees, we stopped to rest. Jakob's face had gone gray with exhaustion. He was too tired to retrieve a loaf of bread from his knapsack. Erik made Jakob eat some of his bread while we rested. Erling and I ate little, for our food supply had dwindled to near nothing. I pretended to take a big draught from our water bottle and handed it to Erling.

"Here. Drink. We have plenty of water," I assured him, fully aware that the other bottle remained empty in the pack. I had noticed that he was coughing more. I had seen him spit blood.

My ski binding had worn through my thin rubber boot heel and my stocking. It raised blisters which had broken. We realized that our hope of reaching the valley below before nightfall grew dim. "The snow has slowed us down," Erik said, folding his map and replacing it in his knapsack's outside pocket. "We must work for every step, when we should be flying down this valley. We'll need to keep close together after dark." He glanced at Jakob, who sat with his eyes closed, ashen-faced.

"Time to go," Erik said, stepping onto his skis. "We'll stop again in an hour." I kept alongside Jakob, bracing him to pull out when his foot stuck in the deep snow. Erik helped Erling pull the unwieldy sled.

Jakob floundered repeating, "Jesus help me, Jesus help me." His praying irritated me. Why had we allowed this self-centered man to come along? He didn't deserve our help. I began to resent Jakob's weakness. "Jesus won't hear your selfish prayer," I finally scolded him. "Pray for us too. You're not the only one who needs help."

I tired quickly trying to haul Jakob along. We crossed a meadow in the late afternoon and Jakob capsized into some deep snow. I worked to extricate him, but he was a dead weight. "Jakob, you must get up!" I cried. "I can't pull you out with no help from you." Jakob said nothing. He just lay in the snow where he fell, looking more dead than alive. I took his arms and pulled with all my strength. He rose out of the snow. Suddenly I lost my balance and pitched forward, plunging deep into the mush. I floundered, trying to brace myself, but my arm sank into the soft snow. I only worked deeper as I struggled. Snow melted in my boots and iced the fiery blisters on my feet. I quit fighting and rested for a moment. It felt so good. I felt brutally tired. The strength had drained from me, like water slipping out of a sink basin. My tongue clung to the roof of my mouth. I was very thirsty, and eating snow failed to satisfy me. I could not go on. An idea came: I would stay here to watch over Jakob while Erik went to town and brought back a rescue party. I drifted and dreamed.

"*Fru* Dahl! Get up!"

Erik's stern voice split my trance.

"I can't, you must go and bring back help."

"No! Get up! You'll die here if you don't."

I opened up my eyes. The sun slammed light onto my retinas. I blinked, dazed.

"It's only six miles longer to Rena, *Fru* Dahl, you can make it. You must make it. Come, get up."

Only six miles! I sat up and Erik yanked me to my feet, holding me steady while I regained my equilibrium.

"Now! Help me with Jakob."

Erik pulled Jakob to a sitting position.

"Come, Jakob, we'll pull you on the sled. Wake up now. We've only a short distance to go."

"Yes. I'll try," Jakob said in a weak whisper.

I used all my strength to help Erik drag Jakob to his feet. We walked him along to where Erling waited. Jakob looked at Erling and refused to ride on the sled, so our bedraggled group moved along, step by step, supporting Jakob and hauling the sled.

I watched with dull gaze as Erling coughed, continuing to spit blood. It's my fault that we're here, I thought. God forgive me.

The rest of the trip passed in a dreamlike blur of exhaustion. Somehow, we reached the Osterdal valley and the crowded town of Rena. We sprawled onto a bench to rest while Erik hunted for a hotel. Like Lillehammer, the little town overflowed with stranded vacationers. Finally, we followed Erik to an inn where he had managed to rouse the sleeping proprietor.

We stumbled into a rustic main room. The innkeeper awaited us, scanning our faces fearfully.

"Are you German?"

"No, *Norske.*"

"You look German." A woman's accusing voice came from behind the counter. A wiry little woman stared at us with suspicious eyes.

"Are you sure? Perhaps you are Nazi," the man persisted. "Where are you from?"

"We are not Nazi!" I retorted. "We are Jehovah's Witness!"

"That's worse!" the little man cried. "Jehovah's Witness cannot stay here."

"Wait. We need your help," Jakob interrupted. "I am not Jehovah's Witness. I am a Christian. I will vouch for these people. They have saved my life today. Please, give us a place--anywhere--so we can rest."

The man shot a glance at his wife and shrugged his shoulders. He led us to a tiny room with two small beds.

"I can sleep on the floor," Jakob said. "I'll sleep anywhere tonight."

"We have money and food stamps," I said, turning to the innkeeper. "Is your dining room open? We must have something to eat."

"No, no. The cook has gone home," the little man said, throwing down the room key on a table and heading for the door.

"But we have had a long journey. We are tired and hungry. Perhaps there is some food we can buy to eat."

The man tried to close the door, but I pushed my weary body in the way.

"No. We have a full house. People stuck here all week. We're out of everything." He pushed past me through the door. "The kitchen is closed."

I talked him down the hall.

"Oh, all right," he said, exasperated. "You can have some ham and potatoes. You may use the kitchen to cook." The man hurried away anxious to be rid of me.

I served the men, then sat down myself. No meal had ever tasted so good. For the first time in our marriage Erling neglected to say "*Takk for maten*" in appreciation for the meal. He and Jakob both fell asleep with their boots on. After sitting, I had no strength to get up again. But the kitchen must be left clean.

Carrying the plates, I passed by a wall mirror, and halted. I peered into the mirror.

"Oooh, no!" I cried. I touched my cheek with my fingers. "My face!" My image in the mirror reflected a face burned brutally. My eyes were blood red, ravaged by the sun. My hair was matted and tangled.

"What would *Mor* think?" flashed through my mind. I put the dishes in the sink, then washed and dried them.

I stumbled down the hall and fell into the bed left for me.

"We can thank God that we are still alive," Jakob said next morning as he pressed several food stamps into Erling's hand. I saw tears in his eyes. I felt a pang of regret--how unkind I was to act so angry with him.

We bid good-bye to Erik, who said nothing of his next destination. We both suspected he planned to join the Resistance, so we let our questions go unspoken. "We would never have made it without you, Erik," Erling said, pumping his hand in farewell.

My gaze slid to the bicycles. I wondered how we would have the strength for several days of hard cycling from this Osterdalen village to Steinkjer. No matter, we must go. Every day's delay witnessed a dwindling of our precious hoard of food stamps. At home, the relatives' farms provided plenty to eat. We couldn't afford another night in the hotel. So, we shouldered our knapsacks and mounted our bikes. Slowly, we eased out of the village and headed into the undulating hills. Erling had purchased maps. We traveled back roads because people told us only the little-used country routes remained open.

"I am anxious to see *Far* and let everyone know we're all right," I told Erling during a late afternoon stop at the summit of a long steep climb. "It will be good to be home. I want to show you everything--my little school, the town square, the *torvet* and the place in the woods we used to call Lovers Park. We won't let this senseless war ruin things for us, Erling. We'll be happy again in Steinkjer."

"Yes. We'll wait there till Oslo is safe again. We can depend on the British for that. They won't forget Norway's help these past years. And then we'll take up our work again. I believe it's needed more than ever now."

Erling's talk of returning to work planted a seed of hope inside me. I caught my breath and felt ready to go. Norway's panoramic views never failed to refresh me. The wide, shimmering expanse of the Glomma River snaked below, with sections of plowed farmland pushing to its very edge. The timber-rich Osterdalen provided ample opportunity for loggers. Some men worked below to break a log jam and we noted their progress.

Late that same day, we sailed down a long, curving road to a narrow valley with a small farm nestled in its green crevice. We slowed down for a herd of cows on the road and had to wind through the animals' bulky forms to pass.

"Who is watching these cows?" I asked. Their udders stretched so full, I thought they would burst. "Perhaps the farmer and his wife are ill. Let's go knock on their door. We can milk their poor cows for them." I laughed. "Too bad we don't have a book to place while we're at it."

The rough-hewn farmhouse door reverberated under our volley of pounding, but no one came to answer. The farm stood deserted. Some chickens pecked disconsolately in the barnyard. The cows lowed in misery.

"There must have been an emergency, a sickness or death in the family," Erling suggested. "There is nothing we can do." He took my arm firmly. "We'd better go on." I stroked one of the cows. "What a shame... it's so strange," I said, reluctant to leave the unhappy animals.

That night, we slept under the trees. As we passed the rolling farms of the fertile Trondelag region next morning, our sense of strangeness grew. On an idyllic spring day new-green meadows and fields stretched in seeming tranquility before us. Rustic farms straddled hilltops and clung to slopes. But every farm stood abandoned, its occupants gone, its animals forlorn and bellowing. We'll ask when we get to Steinkjer, we told each other. *Far* always has the news.

Chapter

Infamy

Something leaped inside me when I saw familiar sights in the rural district south of Steinkjer. I recognized the farms. The fjord sparkled blue far beyond. Soon, we would be safe with *Far*.

"There it is!" I cried. "But what's wrong? Oh, Erling, something's terribly wrong."

We pedaled faster as we neared the town and my eyes flooded with tears. "Dear God, what has happened to Steinkjer?"

"It's been bombed, Ragna. With no mercy. There is nothing left."

We rode our bicycles through Steinkjer's south side. I spoke in dazed shock. "This is our house, Erling. This is where I grew up." The stone foundation gaped at me amid a litter of painted yellow siding boards and broken windows. "Oh, where's *Far*?" I wailed. "Where is my father?"

We went through the rubble of the house half expecting to find *Far* lying injured or dead. *Far* was not there.

Mor's cast iron cookstove rose from the ashes of a burned kitchen.

"Look," I choked through tears. *Mor*'s wedding chair, fashioned from the saddle she rode as a bride, was rocking crazily in a sudden gust of fjord breeze. "Oh, *Mor*! Your things! What will we have to remember you?" I sobbed. I stumbled through the wreckage to get the rocker, but Erling restrained me. "Come, Ragna. We must find your father. We must know if he is all right."

He led me away, coughing in the dust we raised. "My father is 83 years old," I said dully. "How can *Far* have survived this?"

We approached a guard station. A handful of officers in Nazi uniforms eyed us as we came close, walking more slowly with each step. "We are searching for my old father. He is lost," I explained. One of the guards replied in Norwegian--a Norwegian Nazi! "What are *you* doing here?" I burst out. Erling jabbed me. "Oh, I thought I recognized you," I said. "Forgive me."

We picked our way through Steinkjer's ruined streets, walking our bikes amid the rubble. Not a single building escaped without some damage from the attack. My friends' homes lay ruined, boards strewn about, foundation rocks scattered. Some survivors had already used the scrap for shanty and hut shelters. The centuries-old buildings around the town square lay in ashes. The *torvet* lay in ruins with remnants of a vegetable stand punctuating the gray rubble with rotting green.

Beyond the *torvet* and ruined quay we stopped at the cemetery where *Mor*'s grave remained untouched, calm and serene amid the devastation.

"Oh, *Mor*," I cried, falling to my knees. "I'm glad you didn't live to see this!" I laid my face on the cool grass and let the tears flow, just as I had when I sobbed the story of my first heartbreak into *Mor*'s shoulder so many years ago. I dried my eyes and stood up.

"The Germans won't ruin us with this ugly war, Erling. And Steinkjer will rebuild. This isn't the end of Steinkjer or you and me."

. . .

We combed the highland farms and found *Far* next day with relatives on their place above the fjord. He looked hale and strong. We watched happily as he went about his light farm chores. The German war planes had avoided these mountains and people had remained in their homes. We learned that farmers to the south had fled for their lives as the bombers streaked through the sky above them, leaving horse and plow, seed and furrow, cow and calf to hide in the hills. *Far* was discovered very much alive by Nils, a young cousin sent out to search for him. The old man had returned to the ruins of Steinkjer and built a few little huts for villagers. Nils found him making *lefse*, the potato pancakes he loved, over an open fire. As he stirred the heavy potato mixture in the big cookpot, three German soldiers gathered round to watch hungrily. The group grew in size as *Far* began to shape his dough into flat cakes. Soon, *Far* was feeding a crowd of enemy soldiers who had erupted into boisterous talk and sign language to *Far*. "The Germans are people, too,"

Far had explained to young Nils. "We are *Norske*. We don't hate any-one."

Erling and I stayed on the farm almost a month, working in the fields and enjoying the hearty country meals. But we hungered for information on the world outside. We did learn that the British Air Force had landed in Steinkjer and other towns, an attempt to resist invasion forces. The Germans reacted with fierce air attacks on all those communities with British strongholds, bombing them to utter destruction. Neighbors reported that the Germans had overrun all of Norway, that Nazis seized the government in Oslo, that the King had disappeared, whether murdered or still in hiding, no one knew.

We began to wonder what had happened to the headquarters in Oslo. What about Freda and *Tante* Margit? No mail, no telephone, no communication except stories repeated over and over... Erling grew restless and irritable. I tried to mask my growing impatience. Would we be allowed to resume our pioneering work? I certainly was getting nowhere witnessing to my family. The Opdahls disdained the message of truth and in fact had prayed the war would knock some sense into me. I knew they still regarded me as a religious fanatic, an embarrassment, a rebel. All this combined to prompt Erling and me to agree: Time had come for us to move on. We would return to Oslo.

A June sun shone hot the day we left the farm. I kissed *Far*. The seeds we helped to plant had sprouted in the fields, their inner forces propelling the seedlings into lusty green growth under the sun's daily 22-hour barrage of energy. I experienced that same inner compulsion, pushing me forward into the high noon of life. Erling and I said "*Farvel.*"

Almost immediately, we faced the grim consequence of our decision. The roads bucked and bounced us mercilessly. The road's dirt surface was ridged like washboard from the thundering German trucks that roared along the roadways. These monstrous trucks, the highway's only traffic, had reduced the roads to an obstacle course--hard going for cyclists facing a 300-mile trip.

"Erling, look at us. We have dust in our teeth. We're ruining the bicycles. And we're making almost no progress. The trip will take a week to 10 days on good roads. Let's flag down a truck and ask for a ride."

"No! We can't do that, Ragna. If Norwegians see one of our women in the company of German soldiers, they will kidnap her and cut off her hair--or worse. We will ride to Oslo--on our bicycles."

"But I am tired, Erling. The Germans are not going to hurt us.

They're just boys. And all the Norwegian men have joined the underground. They're in hiding, not out here on roads crawling with Nazis ready to scalp countrywomen. Please, Erling, consider my idea. At least we would get to Oslo. This way, I'm not sure."

"You will risk your hair--but I will not. We won't talk of it--enough!"

We rode on in silence. A truck rumbled up behind us. I smiled and waved. A blond boy of eighteen or so leaned out and called, "Good day, *Fraulein*."

Erling looked shocked. I ignored it. "You see?" I demanded. "Just young boys, as harmless as your brothers."

He looked straight ahead. "Please continue riding, Ragna." His lips formed a tight line.

During our lunch stop, I cut thin slices from a small piece of *gammel ost* cheese from the farm. Riding made us ravenous and with stomachs stretched from eating well for a month, we had gobbled up most of our food supply. We still had some flat bread and a little dried herring--but that was all.

The sun rose at 1 a.m. the next morning. Erling and I started riding very early. Our gnawing stomachs and the persistent sunshine drove away sleep. We finished the last bit of food at *middag* time. Food and our strong bodies had kept our energy high for the first few days of battling the rough roads. But now, dirty and exhausted, we both felt weak. Each push of the pedal became an effort. We stopped frequently. Finally, Erling gave in. "All right," he smiled wryly. "You will have your way. We'll see if you keep your hair!"

I wondered now if I had the nerve to stop a German military transport. We stood alongside the road waiting. A truck barrelled noisily toward us. I gulped, my hands frozen to my sides. Later, another truck approached. I stood up and raised a trembling hand.

The truck squealed to a stop, bathing the two of us in road dust. A young man leaned out. "Can we help you?" he inquired in German.

My limping German took us through a request for a ride to Oslo. The two soldiers jumped from the cab and hoisted the bicycles into the truck. "We will be happy to give you a ride." We exchanged courteous remarks, then lapsed into smiles as the truck resumed its deafening journey. When the soldiers stopped for the night, the driver offered me a blanket. We shared a little food.

"These boys are as unhappy about invading Norway as we are," Erling said, staring at his folded hands thoughtfully. "I never believed I'd feel sympathy for the Germans. But they're just like us--

stuck in a bad spot in a bad war and hoping to get home soon."

When we arrived in a cloudy Oslo, we repeated *"Danke schon,"* smiled and nodded, then hurried away on our bicycles to our tiny apartment. We were anxious for news of Freda. Oslo showed no signs of bombing, but the gray harbor disturbed us--no fishing boats or trawlers, no commercial ships or freighters crisscrossed the water. The fjord, usually bobbing with sails, lay somber, even sinister. Just as gloomy were Oslo's streets. People hurried along, with no gay greetings to one another, and no noisy jokes. No children scampered in play along the sidewalks. I shivered in the ghostly breeze. Then we were home. The apartment looked like someone else's, familiar, but somehow alien as we entered. So much had happened. My winter coat still lay across a chair. Light slanted in at the edges of the window shades. The air smelled musty. I sank limp onto the bed. My body flooded with exhaustion as I let go. But my mind burned with unanswered questions. What of Freda? Would she feel deserted by our long absence? What of the headquarters--did the Nazis close it down? Was there food in Oslo? How would we live? My mind marching down a labyrinth of confusing dead end passageways, I closed my eyes. Grimy, sweaty and fully dressed, I lay across my prized wedding quilt and slept.

. . .

Next morning, we approached our beloved headquarters with a mixture of fear and hope. Had the Nazis commandeered the building? Would we be arrested? What had happened to the brothers and sisters? We had to know. The venerable two-story building showed us an impassive face. No sign of activity ruffled its bland features. No cars waited out front. No visitor entered or left. But the window shutters stood open... The sign still hung above the door... Maybe?

Erling turned the door knob. The door opened. No one sat at the reception desk. We tiptoed inside. How would we answer if a soldier questioned us?

"Brother Dahl! And Sister Dahl, how wonderful that you are safe!" A plump gray-haired woman with hair drawn back in a knot hurried toward us from another room.

"Sister Ansted! Then things are well here?"

"Oh, yes! The Nazis are too busy hunting Resistance fighters to come arrest us. So we go on, the same as always, although our book 'Enemies' is banned." She shook her head. "Ah! But let me call the others!"

Soon a group had gathered to welcome us. We all sat in the library with a freshly-brewed pot of coffee, a precious commodity these days. After the greetings, Erling explained about our journey across the mountains from Lillehammer and all that followed.

"But we need to hear your news. We had almost no information on the invasion. What happened in Oslo? Why didn't the army mobilize to beat back the Germans immediately? And where is King Haakon?"

I listened as our excited brothers related news of the last six weeks. Their voices rose till someone cautioned, "Hush" and they continued in low tones.

"Did you hear about the first event of the invasion?" a young brother asked. "A little whaler with only one outdated torpedo fired the first shot--and took an enemy man of war. On April 8, the little fortress at Oscarsborg spotted a German cruiser at the mouth of the Oslofjord. The Oscarsborg soldiers managed to sink the ship. It turned out to be Germany's newest heavy cruiser, the *Blucher*. It sank, drowning thousands of Gestapo and other special intelligence troops trained to organize the occupation of Oslo. Of course, the people on the street are calling it "patriotic." They say that single act of bravery set back the takeover of Oslo long enough for King Haakon and his family to escape."

"*Ja*," exclaimed Sister Ansted. "The Norwegian government had time to get out ahead of the Nazis--government officials, members of the *Storting*, general staff and the gold reserve of the Bank of Norway!"

"But how could a fleet of German ships steaming on open water toward Norway remain undiscovered?" Erling asked ruefully. We all exhanged glances. As Witnesses, we believed the Bible prophecies and expected "wars and rumors of war," especially in these last days. Also, as Witnesses we maintained political neutrality. We found the reaction of our fellow Norwegians a bit ironic.

"Nobody is sure why the attack surprised us, but the Resistance fighters have claimed that one thing is certain. They believe that stupidity and treason played a part," another brother declared. "Earlier on that day, April 8, the British had torpedoed a German transport in Norwegian waters. Twelve hundred men died. Some of those drowned were youngsters, 16 and 17 years old. People say the German boys were blown into the water crying "*Mama*." Survivors told the British they were enroute to Bergen to protect that city against the British. London also radioed Oslo that German war ships had headed north, toward Narvik, the steel-producing center. The

Storting met to consider the emergency, but no warning went out to the people. Church bells did not ring. We all went to bed that night unaware that the Germans landed 15,000 troops in Oslo before dawn on the 9th."

"But I left the headquarters very late that night, after studying in the library," the young man interrupted. "Some men stood on street corners handing out a circular from Vidkun Quisling, the politician. It said a glorious new day was dawning for Norway. Now the people hiss his name, call him a traitor. People say that Quisling invited Hitler to invade Norway so he could become minister-president. To answer your question: Our army mobilized immediately, but Quisling canceled mobilization--and confusion broke out everywhere. Nobody knew what orders to follow. That snake caused the downfall of Norway!"

A young woman spoke up. "We were shocked to see the streets fill with Nazis that first morning. My sister who works at the Grand Hotel told me that business travelers emerged from their rooms in Nazi uniforms. Sailors on commercial ships in the Oslofjord disembarked in Nazi uniforms. And they tell us the same happened everywhere. At Christiansand, an enemy fleet sailed into the harbor under British and French colors. At Narvik, Germans fought in Norwegian uniforms. The country was betrayed from the inside and overrun from the outside. Of course, the people are crying "treachery! and "infamy!"

I remembered Erik heading off to join the Resistance. The gray-haired brother picked up the story:

"We stood on the streets and watched the Nazis march down Karl-Johan Boulevard. We also watched the young men quietly disappear. Soon the Resistance had destroyed railway buildings and managed to prevent German reinforcements from reaching the Western front. In every village, sportsmen and skiers experienced with hunting weapons formed companies and batallions. They fought night and day for three weeks, protecting landing areas for Allied planes, sabotaging German depots, attacking German planes and ground transport. Then, on May 6, Norway surrendered."

"A sad day!" we all agreed. "*Jasaa*, a shame!" But just what the Bible predicts.

"*Ja*, the Allies had no air strength left. The British navy blew up 10 German destroyers in mid-April. These ships carried 2,000 troops ready to occupy Narvik. But you saw what happened when they tried to protect Steinkjer. German war planes reduced those towns to ashes--Andalsnes, Namsos, Mosjoen and Steinkjer--because the

British were there. The British realized they were hopelessly inferior. They pulled out of Trondelag at the end of April and Norway surrendered just over a week later."

Our friends' reports hit us with the rapidity and impact of machine gun fire. We stumbled home, stunned by the news.

. . .

The year 1940 blurred into 1941, punctuated by pain. Friends suffered lack of food, families mourned a dead son, a father was arrested, *Tante* Margit's house commandeered, towns taken over. Norwegians endured hunger, while German officers consumed *Norske* chocolate with *Norske* butter slathered on it. Norwegian fish and fertilizer went to pay German war debts. Norwegians watched their forests logged bare of timber for Germany, our businesses and industries plundered, our public buildings stripped of national treasures.

One night in September, 1941 I waited at nightfall for Erling to return. The neighbors downstairs had pounded on my door earlier with the news: The Germans had declared martial law. Even now I could hear loudspeakers blaring from the corner. German tanks rumbled along the streets. I dared not use a light, for we as yet had no blackout material to cover the windows. Where was Erling? Had he missed the news of martial law and curfew? His food grew cold on the table. I sat in the dark, listening for Erling's step, his voice at the door. I remembered my terror in waiting for *Far* to light the lamp one night long ago. I tried to swallow the dread that rose in my throat. Groping for my Bible, I placed it in my lap. A scripture entered my mind. *Perfect love casts out fear.* I sat quietly in the dark. Today I had something I lacked as a little girl, something I needed as a young woman when death ripped off its mask and stared, jeering, in my face. Today I knew and experienced the protection of Jehovah. I wrapped myself in that comfort the way my grandmother once wrapped herself in her shawl against the northland's winter night. I waited in the dark until my husband came safely home.

Chapter

Nazi Rule

We *Norske* prided ourselves: "With fish and potatoes, we will never starve." In 1942 we discovered that adage to be untrue. The Germans took everything. Their young soldiers came from the embattled motherland undernourished and devoured our food supplies like a Biblical horde of locusts.

I found myself standing in endless lines for food stamps. The wait was hardly worth the few I got (because we had no children) but Erling and I shared the stamps with needy families. One morning I chatted with a mother behind me in the line. Her little daughter reminded me of my Freda. I could see the child's discontent. She was tired of standing, hungry, fidgety. Her coat, once fine, had worn to shreds at the cuff and hem. She had outgrown her little dress. Norwegian mothers had learned to dye blankets and make coats for their children. They sewed their sons Confirmation shirts from white sheets. They sent worn adult garments to the tailors who became adept at transforming old clothes into smaller new ones.

Worn out clothing in itself did not bother me. I came from a poor family. But the effect of this war's deprivation did: The children of Oslo could no longer run and play in the streets freely. They tasted fear for the first time. Freda lost the only home she could remember when *Tante* Margit gave up her home. Freda's ballet lessons ended. (I was so proud. She had danced with the two young princesses, Prince Olav's daughters, in the National Theater. For her it did not seem so special. She went to school with the prince and princesses. All the children expected cakes in the royal lunch sack.

They ate goat cheese and barley bread like the rest.) Freda lost these associations, along with celebrations, summer outings on the fjord, school events, all the fun things, when German boots marched the streets of Oslo. Norwegian children were like little caged birds, they had lost their song.

After I received my stamps, I stepped aside to put them in my bag. "So few?" I heard the mother behind me ask the clerk. "Has our allowance been cut?" She told her little girl that they would have no flour that week. "Oh mother," the girl wailed, "shall we never have white bread again?"

I turned and pressed my food stamps into the mother's hand. "Buy the flour," I urged. "Why should a little girl suffer from this senseless war?"

What incensed me about our children in occupied Norway was not lack of white flour or ballet lessons. Early in 1942 Quisling was appointed Minister-president of Norway under *Reichkommisar* Josef Terboven. As if the ruthless Terboven was not enough--he was "lord over life and death," answerable only to Hitler. Quisling, the Norwegian turncoat, was worse. He began a Nazification of the schools, imposing German "*kultur*" in the classroom. He required all youngsters ages ten to eighteen to join the youth organization of the *Nasjonal Samling* Party, a Nazi puppet group. Teachers received orders to join the Nazi-run teachers association. Teachers protested. They refused to teach from Nazi textbooks. Students resisted. Finally the schools closed. The Nazis arrested 1300 teachers and sent them to the Grini concentration camp. Later, they transported 500 of these teachers to Kirkenes in frigid northern Norway, by boat in slave ship conditions. The rector of the University, a friend of *Tante* Margit, first went to Grini with his professors, then later to the brutal Sachsenhauser camp. When the Nazis took over the churches, the bishops resigned. Yet the Nazis forged on with their bitter determination to break Norway's spirit.

Erling and I tried to be happy during this miserable war. It was not easy. The Germans seized our book *Enemies* and forbade our pioneering. For the first year after invasion they busied themselves chasing down Norwegian resistance fighters and paid little attention to us. Six hundred Jehovah's Witnesses lost their lives in Nazi Germany. When the Nazis launched their inevitable crackdown on our Oslo brotherhood, they confiscated all our publications, then arrested our leader. To our astonishment, he cooperated with the Germans and agreed to disband our group. Many brothers and sisters, afraid of Nazi reprisal, supported him. Just when we needed to stand together, our congregation divided. It was a severe blow to my faith. But my husband held our ground for both him and me. Erling and I vowed we would never stop witnessing. Since they had taken our books, we used our Bibles. If they took our Bibles, we would use our mouths. Others agreed. We made a promise that we would not stop even if we were sent to prison, a spectre that looked more real with each passing day.

A brave brother risked his life to sneak through the German border patrol to Sweden. There he obtained the Swedish *Watchtower* and smuggled it back to Norway where workers translated and distributed the magazine.

All the tension gave me ulcers. I found that truly "all things work together for good for those who love Jehovah," for my doctor prescribed white bread, white flour products and special milk. I received extra ration stamps for these luxuries and shared them with friends.

My ulcers improved, but the situation in Norway worsened. The Germans burned the town of Televag and sent its inhabitants to concentration camps to avenge the deaths of two Gestapo shot while trying to arrest Resistance men. The enemy executed eighteen men at Alesund because they attempted an escape to England. Seven hundred university students were sent to concentration camps, 350 of them to German camps where they worked to fortify German borders. In 1943 the Germans succeeded in forcing the Norwegian puppet court to issue its first death sentence. Many Norwegians were deported, among them several hundred army officers, including men who had turned in their weapons after Norway's surrender, trusting the German promise of amnesty. Otto Ruge, appointed army commander in chief by the king prior to his escape, was sent to a concentration camp. The toll on families was agonizing. Norway grieved.

Our own family suffered when Erling's brother, Harald, died in the Norsk Hydro explosion at Rjukan in the 1943 winter. He had married not long before and his young wife gave birth to their first child soon after his death. While food shortages and blackouts failed to shake us, Harald's death pierced our war-hardened armor. We did not understand the senseless tragedy. We had no idea that the Germans were manufacturing heavy water for atomic bombs at Rjukan. Later, we learned that resistance fighters had penetrated the near-impregnable Norsk Hydro fortress from the mountains, scaling a thirty-foot precipice and evading a heavy German guard to plant explosives. Undaunted by the location at the head of a narrow valley and the fortress' six-layer concrete shell, they demolished the Nazis' sole source of heavy water, developed in the German attempt to produce an atom bomb.

We doubted that Harald ever knew the enormity of the Rjukan project. A year later, the Germans tried to transport their remaining heavy water and plant equipment to Germany. Underground saboteurs blew up the ferry boat they used. Norway's underground claimed it a stunning victory for the free world.

During that Occupation period our hardship magnified under the burden of the coldest winters Norway had known in years.

Oslo escaped bombing during the war except for one nightmare New Years Eve when we thought we would never live to see the New Year. The bombs caused carnage on the tramway but we were never hit. We had blackouts throughout the Occupation. Soldiers patrolled the streets. If they spotted even a flicker of light, they would fire, no questions asked. They believed that traitors lurked everywhere. Erling and I heard of a young man who lit a match one moonless night to find his lock and the right key. A German soldier shot him.

Despite their senseless behavior, we still did not hate the Germans. We talked to them on the street. One day Erling and I picnicked in a grove of trees during a short trip. A German battalion stopped and ate their lunch around us. They did us no harm.

One of the soldiers asked Erling if the nearest town had gasoline. We started a conversation with them. After a while one soldier remarked, "I suppose you Norwegians hate us." The others nodded. But we did not hate the poor soldiers and told them so.

Our own countrymen presented more of a problem. We had to be careful talking to strangers. We never knew when a *Norsk* Judas who would run to the N. S. might eavesdrop, so we had to watch our tongues.

We also kept quiet about our Jewish neighbors. Before Hitler, Norway's population consisted of Norwegians. We saw a few gypsies, but no other foreigners. When the Germans began to harass the Jews, these people flowed out of Germany, Poland and the little countries to Norway for refuge. Now they were wearing stars.

We felt sorry for these persecuted people. A story circulated about an immigrant Jewish peddler who, like the Christ child, could find no place to stay on a cold Norwegian Christmas Eve. Jewish itinerants often sold clothes to the farmers, trudging from farm to farm with their bundles. People gladly bought the clothes and offered the peddler a place to sleep at nightfall. On Christmas Eve, one of these nomad Jewish merchants approached a Norwegian farmhouse. A big wood fire blazed merrily in the stove within. Food piled high on the table. Christmas Eve is even more festive than Christmas Day in Scandinavia. Outside the stars shone brightly and the Northern lights illuminated the horizon. The Jew stared through the window but did not knock, for the wandering sons of Abraham assumed that they were welcome in Norway's Christian homes on any other night--but not on Christmas Eve. So the peddler made his way to the cold stable and covered himself with his bunch of clothes as best he could.

The farmer found his frozen body on Christmas morning.

I knew that my brothers, Jakob and Jens, continued to smuggle Jews over the border to neutral Sweden. They knew their way through the mountains and how to evade the German patrols. My brothers and many like them risked their lives to assist the Jews. Finally, the Germans transported seven or eight hundred remaining Norwegian Jews to Germany. All trace of them was lost. We were afraid to ask questions.

One person who failed to tame her tongue was *Tante* Margit. German-born, she grew incensed with the Nazi treatment of Norwegians. She scolded the soldiers every chance she had for impounding our radios, for taking people's food, for commandeering her home, for taking clothes from her children's backs, for enforcing ridiculous regulations. On May 17, during ironic Independence Day formalities in Oslo, she chided a Nazi officer in public. Freda was at home alone when the call came: *Tante* Margit was arrested in the city.

Imprisonment ruined the doctor's health. She came away gaunt and wasted. Her mental state worried us more than her frailty. Margit had experienced a nervous breakdown as a girl. Her family disapproved of her fiance. He wasn't good enough. When he gave up and married another young woman, Margit went to pieces. Now her depression of younger days returned.

One day she came to visit me at the tiny place where Erling and I lived. I don't believe she had any idea how poor we were. She asked for tea and I found a few leaves at the bottom of a tin. Fortunately they colored the hot water. I don't think she noticed. She had come to ask me a question: "What will we do about Freda when I die?"

In the end Freda, not *Tante* Margit or me, made the decision. She was twelve years old when *Tante* Margit died. I went to her, but could not comfort her. She was tortured with remorse: During a visit with Margit to a cousin's farm, Freda had received a more tempting invitation to go to a friend's place on the seashore. She had felt an inner urging to stay, but went to be with her friends. Freda returned to find *Tante* Margit dead. Her grief was frightening and all the turbulence of her transition to adulthood came to the surface. "Why should you cry?" she raged at me. "I'm the one who loved *Tante* Margit." Then she locked herself in her room and refused to eat. My heart ached for her.

I wakened to her playing the piano at two o'clock in the morning. Per Gynt's passionate music for his lost mother, *Ase's Death*. I can still hear her at the piano, so fluent, so expressive. Her anguish devastated me. I shared her pain but she could not understand that. We did not have that kind of relationship. I did not know what to do. I could not go downstairs to comfort her.

Tante Margit's stepmother offered her gracious home to Freda. She called this woman *Bestemor*. She loved her. Freda could attend a good private school nearby to finish her education.

Freda herself decided. "If I say 'no' to Bestemor she will be unhappy with me. But I will stay with you."

When we tried to fit her things in our cramped apartment, I wondered if Freda wished she could change her mind. We pushed her piano against a wall and it took up the whole room. Erling rigged a curtain for her privacy and fixed a tiny closet in the hall where she could hang her dresses. Space presented a problem, but we had enough food. Erling had taken a job and had a small ration for meat. My father, aware of shortages in the capital, sent meat and eggs from his farm friends around Steinkjer. When Freda stepped on the scales during a school health exam, she was mortified to discover she had gained weight. "Don't give me those goodies you sneak," she implored me. "My friends will think we are *Norske* Nazis."

Erling enjoyed Freda. He often took her side when I acted unfairly to her. She had so little, except the money *Tante* Margit left for her education. Despite her reduced circumstances, she kept her affluent friends. Randi was the closest. I first met Randi when she came running across the school yard in first grade. Both Randi and Freda ski raced. They beat the older racers all through their school years.

The boys Freda grew up with faced a crisis in 1944. The Nazis had introduced compulsory labor service for all young men. In 1944 rumors surfaced that the Germans planned to mobilize Norwegian boys for service on the German army's eastern front. When Vidkun Quisling issued an order for certain age groups to report for labor service, parents and sons panicked. Many young men took to the forest to hide. The Home Front helped boys cross the border to Sweden. They say some 50,000 fled. Very few young men reported for labor duty.

The Nazis grew more cruel, more brutal. Mass arrests. death sentences, home searches and inhuman reprisals for minor offenses became common. Milorg, the Home Front resistance organization, had swelled ranks to 32,000 by mid-1944 and 47,000 by 1945. They used radio stations and couriers to communicate intelligence information to the British, sabotaged military installations, stole tons of military documents, destroyed railway track and bridges and blew up German central office facilities. Despite these valiant efforts, Norway entered 1945 a ravaged country, its resources depleted, its people heavy-hearted. The Nazis were burning the region of Finmark in Norway's arctic north. They burned the entire northland to thwart oncoming Russian troops. Norwegians feared they would cremate the entire country in a satanic fit of destruction before the Allies gained victory.

In Oslo, Erling and I faced a constant threat of arrest as Jehovah's Witnesses. Winter raged bitter and relentless that fifth year of the Occupation. People lost hope. How we managed to survive that grim 1945 winter only Jehovah knows.

Occupation ended as quickly as it began. On May 7, 1945, Germany capitulated to the Allies. Hitler had committed suicide. Josef Terboven followed suit. On May 8, church bells rang all over Norway, a joyous sound I remembered from averted war in my earliest childhood. Jubilation in Oslo rose as Crown Prince Olav returned to the capital from London on May 13. I have a special love for this man. Olav, the three year old prince in his father's arms, remains as one of my earliest memories. He would be crowned King in my lifetime. I rejoiced. Norway's government officials returned on May 30 and finally its beloved King Haakon, on June 7, 1945, five years to the day he left Norway. The whole city turned out, wild with joy, to welcome him.

Norway's merchant marine was devastated, housing was in crisis due to bombed towns and migration to the cities. Finmark and northern Norway smouldered in ruins. Many Norwegians lay dead, and we had no food, but Norway rejoiced to be free again. A spirit of cooperation energized the country as rebuilding began.

· · ·

Freda became a young lady. She grew up in the stringent post-war period, with no money and strict rationing continued. When Freda graduated from high school I did something extravagant to make up for these harsh years. I used some of *Tante* Margit's college fund to stage a lavish party for Freda at Oslo's best hotel. She invited seventeen couples. They danced that night to a fine orchestra in a hall of mirrors. Freda wore a floor length red and white striped evening gown with a black velvet sash. I had to stand in a long line to get the fabric--but seeing her that evening made everything worthwhile. She wore *Tante* Margit's pearls. She glowed. With the shortages, many girls came in their mother's dresses and boys in their father's dress shirts. I baked fruit tarts to add to a beautiful smorgasbord table with its array of open-faced sandwiches and delicacies. The orchestra planned to quit playing at eleven o'clock, but the musicians seemed to enjoy the party as much as the graduates, so they played on. The evening was magnificent, a grand success.

That year Freda turned eighteen and our little family faced some big decisions. Freda had proven herself an Olympic candidate in skiing. She received an offer to train for the Norwegian Olympic team. On its heels came another offer--a skiing scholarship to the University of New Hampshire in America. After considering the two tempting choices, she decided on the University of New Hampshire. Before we knew it, the flurry of packing and errands was over. Freda left for the United States.

Soon her letters brimmed with news of a young man, Sam Langell, whom she married in America a year later, in autumn, 1950. I stood alongside the Oslofjord on her wedding day. Birch trees near the shore showered leaves like golden rain. I looked out toward the ocean, toward the North Sea and the North Atlantic beyond, beaming my energy all the way to a strange place called New Hampshire. Thousands of miles of water separated me and my daughter on that milestone day. I stretched out my arms and sent my love across that expanse. I gazed for a long time at the horizon. Freda had become mine, and Erling's, during the last brief years. Now she was gone, probably forever. I didn't know if I could stand separation once again.

When the Olympic winter games took place in Norway in January, 1952, Freda and Sam traveled to Oslo. We had a wonderful time together. Besides the excitement of the Olympics, Freda shared the triumph of her former teammates and friends. She took Sam up to Holmenkollen, her childhood home. A little electric train whisked them up to the forested winter wonderland with its ski area and beautiful views. They walked, drinking in a panorama of the island-dotted blue fjord and low-lying snow-covered hills beyond. They took the ferry to Dronningen to the yacht club restaurant. Sam was mesmirized by the lights of the city at night and the parade of moving lights on the fjord, a fairyland scene.

Their visit made Erling and me feel more alive than we had in many months. We were sad to see them go.

America held the promise of employment for Erling and an uninterrupted future of cuddling grandbabies for me. Erling's succession of chauffeur-manservant-gardener jobs in various U.S. cities finally led to his labor of love as gardener in "Erling's Park," Denver's beautiful Washington.

Chapter

America!

Erling read Freda's letter aloud. Being a man of leisurely temperament and languid action, he meandered through the letter, savoring each sentence. "Erling. Hurry up! It sounds as if she is pregnant. Read on!"

"I'm getting there. No need to rush," Erling scolded, twinkling his eyes mischievously. "Let's see now. Where was I? Oh, yes."

"So, I went to the doctor yesterday to see about these symptoms and he told me I am pregnant. The baby is due in December."

"A baby! How wonderful!" I hugged Erling. "A grandchild. Oh, Erling, can we go to America when the baby is born? We will have to meet our first grandchild in person."

"I suppose you are already packed, just in case," he chuckled. "But I need to think about it."

Freda will want to make a real home now, I thought. She will need her family things. I decided to send her piano, *Tante* Margit's piano, Freda's heirloom. When I checked into shipping, I found the cost for transport from Oslo to Baltimore, Maryland, U.S.A. would be six hundred *kroner*. Erling reeled. "She could buy a new piano with that money," he groaned. And yet, the young people were settling down to make a real home, to start a family. Freda must have her own piano. After some talking, my kind husband agreed.

When the man came to crate the piano, I had a strong impulse to hide in the box. I'm glad I resisted, for when Freda finally received my surprise weeks later, she had to tell the delivery man to put the piano box back on the truck. She had no room. She and Sam put the piano in storage. I didn't realize how small their place was--one crowded room with a tiny kitchen--no place for a grand piano.

Erling had given in on the piano issue, not because he was a pushover, although he was an easygoing man. He agreed because he cared so much for my happiness. Erling had a sixth sense for others' needs, especially mine. I would call him intuitive. He would turn up with what I needed before I realized the need. He was flexible enough to change his mind if he saw that Freda or I cared deeply about something. And when sending the piano turned out to be a mistake, Erling never brought it up to me. He cared too much to embarrass me that way. You can see why I loved the man.

Of course, I learned to ask the right way, for when Erling put his foot down, no one could be more definite. Then I could see the strength in him, strength that stayed with him from his youth. I respected that strength and avoided pushing him to where he would set his will.

I had changed my mind about wanting to visit America. I wanted to move there, permanently. It would take a master in diplomacy to persuade Erling. I decided to make a try. Since he loved to read, I began bringing him books and articles on America. Jobs abounded in post-war America, we learned. A man like Erling, gifted with gardening ability, could find a position in almost any city. Americans had money, but no real peasant class. They would snap up a man willing to work as a chauffeur, gardener, butler or handyman. We talked about the opportunity to witness in America. People had open minds there. No state church existed to strangle people in its doctrinal grasp. Slowly America emerged in Erling's mind as the fabled "land of opportunity."

The catalyst came when Freda gave birth to a girl. They named her Astrid. Sam adored the baby. Freda sent pictures of the newborn who looked sweet as a tiny rosebud. Erling and I made plans to go to America.

. . .

We stood against the rail of the ocean liner Oslofjord. Tears streamed down my cheeks, watering the armload of flowers I held. My brother, Kristoffer, along with dozens of friends, relatives and Witness brethren, waved from the pier. A brass band played the Norwegian national anthem. Fireboats sent plumes of water skyward. Dozens of little boats, white sails bobbing, waited to escort us out into the fjord. I held Erling's hand and sobbed.

The giant ship eased away from the dock. I felt a little queasy, probably from the excitement, but continued to wave frantically to loved ones I might never see again. We passed small islands where bathers on shore, their little boats beached nearby, signaled *bon voyage* with their towels. Finally, our friends melted into a blur of moving humanity. I looked up at Erling with wet eyes. "We're on our way," he cried. "America, here we come!"

We we off to explore the ship. A library, game room, lounges, the ship's dining room. A small *bon voyage* party attracted passengers to the salon. When a white-jacketed waiter offered us hors d'oevres from a silver tray resplendent with fancy canapes, my stomach turned.

"Erling, I'll need to go back to our stateroom," I announced weakly.

For the next nine days, while Erling stuffed himself on delicacies from the ship's groaning board, played cards, sunned himself on a deck chair, beat other passengers at shuffleboard and listened to the wonderful orchestra after dinner, I lay sick. The ship rolled, rose and sank. It seesawed. It tossed and pitched. The motor throbbed like a giant pulse. I dreamed I was a captive on a stomach-churning carnival ride. The stateroom, airless and dank, became my prison cell. A small portable fan kept me alive.

Happy to leave for America at age 53, I smiled for a passport picture.

Erling, on the other hand, enjoyed himself to the hilt. He popped in with a cheery "How are you?" every hour or two. I moaned. He had happened on a bridge game with a group of rich Americans. Erling played expert bridge and relished this opportunity to shine.

When I could bring myself to focus, I looked at my new shipboard clothes swaying on their hangers. It galled me to see my blue velvet dinner dress unworn. I determined to get better, just to wear that dress.

The sea shone smooth as glass the night of the Captain's dinner. I rose like a phoenix from the ashes of my undersized sickbed and rouged my gray cheeks. I felt better once I had the blue dress on. "When you introduce me to your American friends," I told Erling, "they'll say, 'Oh! You're married? We didn't know.'"

It was the evening I had dreamed of, only had I expected nine of them. Elegantly dressed passengers strolled the deck basking in the warm summer air as a fiery sun dipped into the ocean horizon. I held Erling's arm. I was proud of my handsome husband, tall, tanned and lithe. We entered the dining room, resplendent with flowers, white linen, gleaming silver.

I made it through the soup course. The perfume from the floral arrangement set me off. Giving a polite "excuse me" smile to Erling's Americans, I careened to the dark solace of my stateroom.

I had to summon the energy to pack as we neared New York harbor. Luckily I had never really unpacked. Above on the deck, Erling steadied me with his strong arm. The July night gathered darkness. As we approached, we saw the city dazzling like a jewel cage in Topkapi Palace. I stared fascinated at the skyscraping lighted buildings, the star-studded arterials, moving chains of headlights.

"Oh, no..." Erling groaned. "That's New York?"

"What's wrong, dear?"

"Look at that traffic! I'll never be able to drive in America. It's ten o'clock. Everyone should be in bed, and it's a madhouse!"

Sam found us in the melee. We had never seen such crowds, such confusion, but Sam handled everything, even customs, calmly. Two days later, we were admiring our seven-month old grandchild in Baltimore, Maryland.

Erling breathed relief, glad to be out of New York City.

I cuddled little Astrid, an activity I planned to do nonstop for a long time.

"Mother," Freda said, "we've got you a job. You start tomorrow. Isn't it wonderful?"

I groaned silently.

"There's a Jewish family nearby that needs a housekeeper, only for six weeks. The parents leave for Europe on Thursday and you'll take care of their teenagers and run the house." I gazed into Astrid's angel eyes. "And here I thought we were going to play," I exclaimed in a cheerful grandmotherly voice. "Why that's wonderful, dear," I said fondly to Freda. "We knew jobs would be waiting for us here in America."

Erling spent the next eight weeks looking for a job. No luck. Part of the problem, of course, was that he spoke no English. He had taken an English class in Norway before we left but the language just plain baffled him. Finally a Jewish hospital hired him as a handyman. When my housekeeping position ended, I got a job babysitting a child Astrid's age. My strong Norwegian legs, tuned by Norway's ever-present hills, served me well. On Sam's bicycle, I rode ten miles daily to and from my job.

We discovered Americans to be friendly and open. We wanted to begin our pioneering work as quickly as possible. The problem was that I found myself in a dither when we went door to door, for Erling constantly asked in Norwegian, "What did he say? What are you talking about?" Then I must interrupt my witness and explain to him. This happened at home (we still stayed at Freda's apartment) at parties, pioneering, everywhere. I got so tired of repeating everything. I tried to teach Erling some English. He practiced on Freda and Sam. To me, he was hopeless. But Erling remained undaunted. One day he announced that he would give the witness on our next visit.

We started on a tree-lined street with neat houses. As the housewife sat us in the living room, we noticed the family had a television set. She turned it on to show us how it worked. We were amazed. Erling had introduced us with a few phrases heavily laced with Norwegian which he had written down on little slips of paper. The lady did not seem to mind. He haltingly told her of the good news from the Bible, about Christ's reign on earth, no wars, no sickness, no death. She smiled brightly the whole time. I had the idea she understood not one word of his *Norsk*-English gibberish. "Please don't listen just to my message," Erling said in incomprehensible English. "The Bible tells the story better than any words of mine can."

He's right about that, I thought. The lady gave a beatific smile. Erling picked up his Bible and began to read Isaiah--in Norwegian. He got so caught up in the passage, he didn't realize his mistake. I tried to catch his eye. He read on, bold, fluent, eloquent. I tugged on his pants leg. He scowled. The lady continued to smile.

When Erling finished, there was a silence. He looked satisfied. The lady stood up, smiling. "Thank you, thank you very much," she said brightly, ushering us to the door. For once, I was speechless. Erling began to look a little puzzled. Before we knew it we were out on the sidewalk.

"You read in Norwegian," I hissed as we went through the picket fence gate.

"I did?" he said. "No wonder I sounded so good!"

After a year, Sam's company transferred him to a new job in Stamford, Connecticut. Erling and I followed. We liked Stamford. Erling landed a job as a chauffeur for a rich widow. He grinned when I told him he looked smart in his uniform. He also cared for the widow's garden. His wizardry with flowers compensated for his still-balky English. We congratulated ourselves. Domestic service in the U. S. proved to be a plum job.

After our second grandchild, Elisa, was born, Erling and I teamed up to work as cook and chauffeur-butler for a wealthy Stamford family. We enjoyed being together and I could help Erling with the language.

I served dinner every evening at seven o'clock. Erling helped to lay the table after he put the car away from Mr. Novograd's trip home. Later, we carefully did the dishes, heirloom china. Our days went like clockwork.

Until April, that is. We had joined a Jehovah's Witness congregation in Stamford. The year's most important event occurs on the night of Christ's Last Supper. We hold a Memorial meeting. Every member around the globe attends this meeting on that evening.

But what to do about dinner? Erling and I fretted about this for days. We decided on a simple solution. Erling would just ask the family to eat their dinner early, at five o'clock. We would dress in our good clothes, put our uniforms on over the good outfits and serve the meal. Then we would race our aging auto to the Kingdom Hall and just make the service.

At five o'clock, looking a little bunchy in our uniforms, we served a carved standing rib roast, new potatoes, peas, molded cherry salad, wine and fruit juice. Nobody came.

I gave Erling a look. "Did you ask them?"

"*Ja, ja.* Don't fuss now. They'll be along."

We waited. Still no family. I felt my long-dormant ulcer kicking up.

"What did they say when you asked them? Did they say yes?"

"*Ja!* They said yes. Don't worry now, Ragna."

I fumed. What could be keeping them? The food was getting cold. Should we just leave? Finally, I strode into the library and surprised Mr. and Mrs. Novograd signing papers at their desk. I burst in without knocking.

"The food is on the table," I announced in a tense voice. *"Will you eat?"*

Mrs. Novograd jumped. "Excuse me?"

"You must eat your dinner before it is ruined!" I exclaimed wildly. I hate to be late, and to be late for the Memorial meeting is unthinkable.

"But Ragna, it is two hours early." She stopped. "Oh, Roger, that's what Erling tried to explain to us this morning. Of course, Ragna. If you have served the food, we will dine. You may expect us in a few minutes, after we call the children and freshen up.

Oh, dear! Surely we will be dismissed over this. I didn't care, I told myself recklessly. We *must* be at the Memorial.

We got there, not without frustration at the pokey car and perspiration over the ticking clock, just when the prayer began. We drove home wondering if we still had jobs. We found a reassuring note from Mrs. Novograd in the kitchen. At midnight, we were washing pots and pans, feeling grateful.

Karin was born in 1956, when Astrid was four years old and Elisa two. That is the year the doctors told me I had cancer. The disease had spread too far for surgery, the specialist said. They told me I must come to the hospital for cobalt treatments. After the initial shock, I did not worry. My life is in Jehovah's hands. When Erling took me to the hospital, the doctors found me knitting socks for Astrid. "I refuse to have cancer," I informed the doctor. "I'll be out of here before your stethoscope gets cold."

The doctor looked at Erling as if to say, "Is she mad?" Cancer in 1956 usually ended in death.

Erling threw up his big hands. "My wife is the world's biggest optimist," he laughed. "And the most determined. If anyone can stand up to cancer, she can."

The doctor shook his head. I think he wanted to recommend a psychiatrist. I took the cobalt treatments. In the treatment room I knit socks and mittens, enough for the whole family.

The next year found me on my way to Norway, a vacation to visit my family. I had no more cancer. I was fifty-seven years old and never felt so alive. I loved visiting my beautiful Norway again. The mountains and fjords were more beautiful than I remembered. But I hurried back to America. I missed my grandchildren.

Freda coaches daughters (l. to r.) Katie, Karin, Ingrid in family music fest.

Happiest when I could babysit, I spent every free moment with these precious little girls. I walked them to the forest to examine all that grew there and to watch for animals. I taught them a Norwegian prayer which we said after stories at bedtime. "Tell us one more story, *Mormor*, and we'll go to sleep right away," they would beg. Their favorites were stories about the New World.

"Three little sisters were lost in the woods," I would begin. "They got so tired of walking. And by dinner time, they felt very hungry. It grew dark, and cold. Suddenly they heard growling and crashing in the black forest. A big, scary bear appeared."

The little ones shrieked. "Mormor!" Astrid said. "This is the New World."

"So it is," I smiled.

"The big bear reared up on his strong hind legs and said, 'My, my, it is very late for three little girls to be out at night. Can I help you?'

"'We're lost, Mr. Bear' said the eldest sister. 'And we're so hungry.'

"'Come, eat some of my berries,' the bear invited. After they ate, he motioned them to climb upon his back. 'I'll take you to the river,' he said kindly. 'Your parents are there searching for you.'

"The bear walked very gently on all fours, careful not to jolt the three sisters clinging to his furry shoulders, and carried them safe and sound through the dark forest to their mother and father."

I shared Bible stories with my granddaughters and read them scriptures on the Resurrection. But I had to be careful because their parents did not share my enthusiasm for my religion. The girls had a good foundation in the Bible, for Sam took them to the Methodist Church.

We lived in Stamford for seven years. Sam accepted a second transfer, this time to Denver, Colorado, a wonderful city with people even friendlier that those in the East. Erling and I liked Denver. We skied in the nearby mountains and enjoyed the cool, dry climate. My husband became a gardener for the Denver Parks Department, creating beautiful flowerbed displays admired by many, especially in popular Washington Park. When Sam and Freda later moved to Atlanta and then to Cincinnati, Erling and I stayed in Denver.

Karin, the youngest, turned seven in 1963, the year Freda and Sam gave us a fourth beautiful granddaughter, Ingrid. Katie, fifth and last, was born in 1965.

Each child had her own distinct personality. Astrid was a little princess, gentle and full of grace. She was born a lady. She could be definite, especially when people called her grandfather (her "*Morfar*") by his Christian name. "That's not Erling," she insisted, "that's Morfy."

Elisa, the maverick, grew up resisting the expectations of others. When she giggled at Astrid's attempts to do the splits in dance class, the teacher said, "Elisa, let us see you do it better." Elisa shrugged. "Who cares?" she replied. Despite our separations during her elementary years, she loved me dearly. When I visited, she would run in the house from school and throw herself into my arms like we had been together yesterday.

Karin was a little rascal. She refused to let anyone help her. She could, and did, help herself. Brimming with life, Karin stood ready to try anything. Sam had to build a fence to keep her in the yard. As a tiny girl, she climbed a trash can and jumped over the fence into the snow. She pulled her sled over and rode it down a steep overhang, landing in a terrible fall that practically slit her throat. For years the scar remained as a reminder.

Ingrid and Katie grew up on skis in the Colorado mountains. Both excelled at winter sports. Freda and Sam had settled their family in Summit County, Colorado, a mountain ski resort area situated beneath the Continental Divide 75 miles west of Denver. Ingrid and Katie attended school there. Both played band instruments, Ingrid the oboe and Katie the flute. Both earned high academic honors.

Now all of us, three generations, enjoyed skiing together, just as we would have in Norway. Erling and I drove up to the mountains to join our family in several citizens' cross country ski races. The *Denver Post* published a photo story on me and my family in February 1973 when I won the Keystone Cross Country Caper race in my senior division at 73 years of age. The reporter asked, "How can you do this?" I gave him my secret. "I have a fountain of youth, something inside that gives me joy."

(Actually, I raced in the Keystone event six years running. I took home two gold medals, one silver and three bronze medals. They called me a race horse because I won all the races, as my father did racing horses many years ago.)

I looked at our pictures in the *Denver Post*. Erling stood erect on his skis, still slim and athletic. I held up my ski poles in victory. The experience climaxed two wonderful decades in the United States. Erling and I talked on the drive back to Denver. The snow-covered mountain scenery reminded us of Norway. We agreed that we were happy we came to America. We had shared our grandchildren's growing up years. As we dropped down through rolling foothills toward the city, we lapsed into silence. We felt happy and fulfilled.

Winning the Keystone Caper ski race (left) and rejoicing with the whole family (below), we cherished happy moments together. Back row: Erling, Sam, Ragna, Karin, Ingrid, Elisa, Astrid. Kneeling is Freda with Katie.

Chapter

A Time to Weep

It is strange... the jangle of a telephone can rip your heart like a razor... the ring can explode in your mind, leaving chaos... a single urgent sound can shatter a family into a group of broken individuals.

The phone rang on a late summer day. When Sam answered, the man on the telephone identified himself as a sheriff's officer from Alaska, where Astrid and her fiance, Sky, had gone for a vacation.

His words battered Sam the way a training ball is buffeted by a prize fighter's blows. Astrid's plane had gone down. Her flight from Juneau to Anchorage with Sky and friends had ended with engine failure over the waters of Yakutat Bay. One body had washed up on shore.

The officer said, "I'm sorry, Sir." Sam choked out a "thank you" and let the phone fall from his hand. He faced the agonizing job of telling Freda and the girls.

I believe that grief ricochets--it hurts more when you see pain reflected in your loved ones. Then their misery magnifies because you hurt--a ghastly game of volley and serve.

"No! No, this can't be true. It's a mistake," I remember crying when Freda called me later. "It is true, Mother," Freda insisted woodenly. "Sam is leaving in the morning for Alaska. If you ever have prayed to your God, now is the time to do it."

I talked with her, trying to offer comfort. I got the feeling that she heard me but that nothing really registered. I think Freda was in shock. The body is wise that way. Shock cushions the blow. I know.

Yakutat Bay

I am no stranger to death.

Erling and I cried together. We thought of Sam, alone on that long flight to Alaska. The flight would be torture. How Sam adored his precious Astrid!

Freda sat by the phone for four days. Friends came and went. She remained calm (or numb perhaps). The wait was agony. Search parties, volunteers from the Yakutat communities, had combed beaches and islands. They faced a real challenge. The bay stretched on endlessly. The search could go on for weeks. Finally, Freda could stand it no longer. As a skier and sportswoman, she was fit for the rescue effort. She insisted that she had enough adrenalin energy to run up Mt. McKinley if necessary. I gave her my Mastercard for air tickets. A friend packed her suitcase. She left the next morning, planning to arrive in Alaska late on the fifth day of the search. All I could say was "God help you."

Erling and I stayed with the girls that Labor Day weekend. News from Alaska offered little hope. We learned that the authorities did not expect to find Astrid and Sky alive. We hung in limbo.

I tried to grocery shop and found myself reaching for some new crop Colorado peaches for Astrid. Her favorite fruit. My mind was in such chaos I couldn't decide what foods to pick from the shelves. I came home with almost nothing in my sack. We half expected Astrid to walk in the door, tanned and smiling, and tell us it was all a crazy mistake.

Then the phone rang again. It was Sam. They had found Astrid's body on the beach.

Ingrid stood by the telephone, demanding "What did Dad say? What's happening?"

I hesitated. "They found her, my darling," I said. "She is dead."

"No! No!" Ingrid screamed. "It can't be. It's not Astrid. Oh, no!"

I took her in my arms, trying to hug away the hurt, wishing I could use my body as a shield to block this pain from reaching her. We wept together. Katie became hysterical when she heard the news. I felt helpless. When they were little, I could kiss away the hurt and distract them with a little folk song. This hurt pierced too deep for a grandmother's comfort.

We knew little of what Freda and Sam were going through. When Freda finally returned, I asked her for details of the search. What she told me broke my heart.

Freda explained, with tears, that by the twelfth day, the day she found the body, they knew Astrid had died. What they wanted most was to find her, to bring her body back home. They planned to scour the entire Yakutat basin until they did.

Weeping, Freda struggled to tell me everything that had happened. She had struck northward from their latest camp that day. The local high school principal accompanied her. Sam had taken a motorboat to another island to search. Not twenty minutes elapsed before Freda sighted a body. She ran along the beach. It was a woman.

"Astrid!" she cried as her knees hit the sand. "Oh, God, my child is dead. My baby, my Astrid. Oh, God!"

Though the body was bloated from almost two weeks in the water, Freda said she knew instantly it was Astrid. Details contradicted that certainty--but she ignored them. Little things like the hands... Astrid kept her lovely nails manicured and polished. These nails looked stubby. The body had no earrings, unlike Astrid who always looked so finished, so polished. The high laced boots seemed wrong... not her style, probably borrowed.

Freda described the scene of her ordeal. Her story scraped a raw wound on my own heart, but I had to hear her out. She sat down on the beach with the body while her companion went to locate the others. I imagine her engulfed by the beauty of the surrounding wilderness. Staggering, saw-toothed St. Elias mountains plunged from 18,000 feet to the bay. Pure water, iced by the magnificent Malaspina Glacier flowing into the bay in the distance, lapped on the woodland beach. Tiny islands rose like pincushions stuck with pointy pine trees. Nature mocked Freda with the irony of this North American Eden, an open-air mausoleum for her dead child.

Freda said she was not there on the beach alone. God was there with her. He listened like a patient father as she screamed again and again, "WHY?"

The rescue party brought a boat. Sam and Freda watched workers put their firstborn into a body bag and lift her into the open launch. They hurried, for clouds had rolled in, threatening rain. The trip though Yakutat Bay waters to the tiny airport seemed endless. As if nature gathered her forces to orchestrate Freda and Sam's grief, the storm began with thunder, lightning and a heavy downpour. They hunched over in the skiff, drenched, desolate, exhausted now that the search was over. They tried to encourage one another with a single consoling fact: They had found Astrid's body and were bringing her home.

They flew to Juneau, heavy rain buffeting the tiny plane. There, local authorities examined the body. They delivered devastating news. The body was someone else. Not Astrid. Officials later identified it as the pilot's girlfriend.

Their only comfort evaporated before their eyes, plunging Freda and Sam into new depths of sorrow. How do two people absorb this kind of blow?

Sam announced he would go back to Yakutat. Freda urged him to reconsider. They had four living daughters at home needing Mom and Dad. Little hope remained for finding Astrid. Most everyone had concluded she, Sky and the other young people had been trapped in the plane as it sank into the isolated, mountain-rimmed bay.

Astrid! My heart cried out to her in that cold watery grave. We had never said goodbye.

. . .

Grief is like a battering ram. It assaults with a barrage of emotions till you are raw, bruised, bloodied. It began with shock and denial, then, for me, moved into frustration. I felt so helpless. "I wish I could help search," I told Erling. If only I could comfort Freda and Sam. I want to *do* something!"

I felt helpless because I had something I could hold onto--my strong belief about death and resurrection. I knew I would have a joyous reunion with Astrid in the new world. But I could not share this comfort with my grieving family. They could not accept it. My worst pain was to see Freda and Sam's sorrow and not be able to console them. They didn't want to hear my Bible talk and I respected their wishes.

Every one of us suffered guilt. We never really told her how precious she was to us. I cherished my beautiful granddaughter more than anything in this world. I would have been more than willing to give my life for hers. Did I show it? I should have written a note more often, called her, sent cookies. We all shared our sadness about not spending more time with Astrid during the busy summer. Why hadn't I taken time to say what was most important: "Astrid, I love you."

Something inside me numbed. I could have raged with Freda at the careless pilot for not maintaining his engines. I could have resented poor, dead Sky--why didn't he take care of our Astrid? I could have been angry at myself for grieving despite my belief in the coming resurrection--it was almost a sacrilege. I did not feel those things. God knows that losing a child is different than, more agonizing than, any other kind of death. I could have screamed, like Ingrid, at the waste. Had I tried, nothing would have come out. I was speechless. It is unnatural for a beautiful young woman to die with a whole life ahead of her. Something died in me.

Slogging through this swamp of unexpressed misery, I still knew in the deepest part of me that I would see Astrid again. I thought of it over and over. I would embrace her, smiling and happy, in the restored earth. I know that Astrid only sleeps now. She awaits her entry into a happy, cleansed earth, where peace, truth and life with no more tears or death will reign. Despite the terrible tragedy of her death, I held on to this truth. I could go on.

Freda and the girls did not have this consolation. Their grief was almost too much for me to bear. One day something triggered the tears again. Freda was weeping so, that I thought we could go no deeper in this mourning. Sobbing on her neck, I said, "Freda, please, please let me show you something from the Bible. Let me show you why God permitted such a terrible thing. Will you get your Bible, Freda. . . for me?

To my surprise, she went to her bedroom and brought back her Bible. What's more, she called Ingrid and Katie to come and listen. The heaviness lifted from me. We started with Romans 5:12 which explains how when Adam sinned, sin and death entered the world that God had created as good. ". . .by one man sin entered into the world, and death by sin. . ."

"Jehovah God didn't make a world of sin, sickness and death," I told them. Ecclesiastes 9:12 tells us that unforseen things happen to us all, "for man knoweth not his time." Death spares no one. Because evil entered the world with Adam's sin, death snares the innocent like "a fish caught in a net or a bird trapped in a snare," the Bible says.

But Jehovah has a plan, I smiled, looking at Katie's tear-furrowed face. "One day Jesus will call Astrid and wake her from her death-sleep. He will call her to the new world I told you about as a little girl during our bedtime stories.

Jesus himself promised that Astrid will rise. In John 5:28 Jesus says, ". . .a time is coming when all who are in their graves will hear his voice and come out--those who have done good will rise to life."

I asked Ingrid to read from the Book of Revelation, chapter 20, verse 4. Her true young voice sang out my favorite words, "And God shall wipe away all tears from their eyes; and there shall be no more death, neither sorrow nor crying, neither shall there be any more pain, for the former things are passed away."

The children looked at me and promised to remember these things. Later I talked more with Freda. We both mourned Astrid's burial in the icy waters of that remote Alaskan bay. I read Revelation 20:13 that says, "The sea gave up the dead which were in it." Freda underlined that verse in her Bible.

I was satisfied.

Over the months Freda and the girls wept until there were no more tears. But not Sam. Sam never cried. Tears not shed never dry up. They just change form inside, like water that turns to ice when winter comes.

Every time one of the girls went somewhere, we were crazy with worry. When Karin traveled back to New Hampshire with Elise, we were ill at ease. We tried to hide our anxiety. The girls needed to go on with their lives.

Healing is full of ups and downs. One day you wake to sunshine and feel like life is beginning again. The next day something small triggers an explosion of sadness. Recovery comes in a sweet leap-- then you slide back into grief again. We got through the winter. Happy news came in the springtime. Karin planned to be married in September. She could hardly wait for me to meet her Edward.

As the months passed Karin's letters from school brimmed with plans for her wedding. We would not see her beforehand because she needed to stay in New Hampshire for the summer. Karin and Edward planned to come home just before the big day. A talented artist, Karin sketched a favorite mountain scene for her wedding invitations.

We used it on the funeral stationery.

The telephone rang at midnight this time, exploding our new-found peace. Freda sat late at her table addressing Karin's wedding invitations. From New Hampshire, Elise's voice came over the line. "Mother," she cried, "Karin is gone."

"Has she run away?" Freda asked. "Scared to go through with the wedding?"

"No, she's, she's..." Lise broke into uncontrollable sobbing. A police officer took the phone. "There's been an accident. Your daughter was killed instantly." Freda could hear Lise weeping in the background.

"Oh, God, no. No. Please, no." Freda screamed.

They waited until morning to call me.

Erling and I wailed and wept. How could we keep our sanity? How could we go on in the face of such tragedy? How can a family lose two cherished daughters and survive?

Karin, our precious, vibrant Karin... gone. I felt the need to talk about her to everyone, anyone. People must know what we lost.

She made us all alive. Karin... warm, sensitive, outgoing to people. She lived intensely, grabbed all of life, didn't want to miss anything. Oh, how we enjoyed her as a child! She wanted to try everying. We laughed at her intensity, the bigness of her desires and dreams. Later, she attended college for three years without choosing a major--not because she drifted. No, Karin was motived, an achiever. She felt torn in choosing among the many fields she liked. Karin, our all around top athlete, stood out in tennis and skiing, but she excelled in gymnastics. Though competitive, fun and sports-loving, she was fresh and feminine. She loved the dainty things we gave her.

Karin's real gift lay in the field of art. She displayed creativity from the time she first held a crayon. She reminded me of my nephew, Jacob Weideman, now a famous European artist. I remember the wonderful dwarf she sculpted in eighth grade. Alive with whimsy, the piece revealed serious talent. Her wire figures, a dancing couple made later, expressed joyous movement in every inch.

Gifted, alive, exuberant, yet balanced, calm, conscientious--that was Karin, the second grandchild we lost.

Again, Sam boarded a plane to claim a daughter's body. Lise, our strong-willed one, had broken the hospital code, demanding to see Karin's crushed body, refusing to be swayed until officials gave in. She wanted her chance to say goodbye. Sam arranged a funeral service in the East, then brought Karin's body home.

We gathered at the Denver airport to watch Karin's Edward step off the plane with her casket. The scene tore me apart. I began to sob. I had waited with joy to see the bridal couple step off the airplane together. It was my happy dream. But not this way. Not this way.

Freda and I had already gone, with tears, to secure Karin's gravesite in the Dillon cemetery. She sleeps there now, amid the scented pines, beneath the guardian mountains she loved.

"Death is so brutal, Mother," Freda told me that week after the burial. It is true. Death is a butcher of lives, dreams, youth.

We were past talking. We labored alone in our grief. In the nightmare of torment, I found solace in the scriptures once more.

Karin died in 1978, just one year after Astrid's death. Erling's health began to fail in 1981. He had suffered an attack of rheumatic fever as a child. We never knew the damage it did until his last years. He never aged. His distinguished David Niven type looks stayed with him till nearly the end. Erling experienced a series of heart attacks, each one weakening him further. He died in 1983 at age 74.

His death left a gaping void in my life. We did everything together. When I made *lefse*, Erling stirred the heavy potato mixture as it simmered. We pioneered together, skied together, traveled together, played together, worked together. He began by carrying my book boxes forty-five years ago. He helped me to carry every burden life brought thereafter. I cannot get over missing him.

The winter of Erling's death stretched on endlessly, long and dark like the Norwegian winters of my youth. I couldn't get warm that winter. I would wrap myself in a quilt and doze in a chair by my heater, reluctant to go to my cold bed. I dreamed over and over again of Norway, waking up alone in the dark and not knowing if it was morning or midnight. I was little and the phantom wind off the fjord moaned, frightening me. Sometimes it gusted and buffeted the house like a raging spirit, shaking my window. Where was *Mor? Far?* My sisters? The blackness gathered and I groped about the quilt, feeling for the warm, sleepy bodies of my sisters. Then I sucked in my breath and woke up. I realized I was alone in the dark.

I learned a way to dispel the darkness. When I awake, I turn on the light and reach for Erling's Bible, the Norwegian one. He has marked many places describing the New Earth. Revelation 21:3-5 was his favorite scripture. I read the words slowly. "Then I saw a new heaven and a new earth ... death shall be no more, neither shall there be mourning nor crying nor pain any more, for the former things have passed away." God proclaims, "Behold, I make all things new."

I believe my loved ones will rise and return to a cleansed earth. All people will form one happy family governed by our heavenly Father. Soon all sadness will cease. We will enjoy this paradise in radiant health, with total security and peace in a prosperous, Eden-like earth. Absorbing work will occupy men and women renewed to youthful vitality in a world where harmony between humans and animals, humans and nature, is restored.

This faith gives me strength to continue to live.

At 86, I delight in skiing, both alpine with Freda (l.) and nordic alone (r.).

Chapter

Beginning Today

I saw a mountain pasque flower the other day. I bent down to sniff it and ran my finger over the pale blue fuzz inside the cup formed by the petals. It is spring and my sense of awe has returned.

I miss the sound of Erling's voice, his touch. But I am learning to fill up my senses. A bird song bids me good morning. Wind and rain caress my skin. I feast on the sight of a new baby or the Front Range horizon. My own wrinkles have become beautiful for they are the shorthand of my life. I love the smells around me, fresh coffee, my bed sheets fresh-air dried and warm from the sun, the pine and wild rose scent of Freda's mountain garden.

I can be alone now. I am making cranberry-apple preserves to give to my friends. I am tanning my legs in the sunshine on my balcony. Despite my eighty-four years I still walk two miles every other morning and jump rope every afternoon. I skied last winter with Freda, both cross country and downhill. The weather turned bitter for our alpine ski day, a thirty-five below zero wind chill. The cold does not bother me. I am Norsk.

When I look in the mirror, I see an old woman. But inside I am young and alive. I have learned that we do not honor the dead by dying with them.

After Erling died, my poet spirit tickled me. I began to write, furiously at first, the story of my life's happenings. Often I awoke at night with a memory to add. Then I turned on my lamp to scribble until that experience, too, was committed to paper. My memory is photographic. I can still see and describe what *Farfar* wore the day he gave me my first sled. I can picture little Prince Olav on that historic railway visit to Steinkjer in 1906 as clearly as if it happened this morning. When my story is finished, I will give it to a professional writer to rewrite and expand. In Norwegian, I could write the book myself, but in English I need help.

I like to be independent. This year, when the State of Colorado required me to take a driver's test, I worried. What if they tell me I can no longer drive my car? I need to drive to live my life. I drive to the mountains, to meetings, to visit my friends. When the officer called my name after the test, he informed me that--yes!--I passed. I threw my arms around him and hugged the burly man, badge, uniform, cap and all. He looked a bit shaken but who am I to contain my joy? Now that I am an old woman, I am free to do as I please. I hugged the mailman last week. In the Norway of my youth that would cause a scandal. A man would visit in the same room with a young woman and was forbidden by etiquette to acknowledge her presence. And she him. I start up conversations with people on the street, old people, teenagers, anyone.

I admit that I am talkative. It helps me in my witnessing. I still go door to door with my books and pamphlets every other morning. I can't stop witnessing. I have done this for more than fifty-five years. Freda gave me "the eyes" at a dinner party recently because she caught me explaining to the nice man next to me about the New World. I got her message. "I can't talk now," I hissed. "Give me your address and I will send you a book to answer your question." What could I do? He asked me outright, "How can we be happy when the world is so bad?" Of course, I had promised myself not to witness that night. The Bible says there is a time to sow and a time to reap, a time to talk and a time to be quiet. I was being quiet. Sometimes that works better than other times.

When the time comes to talk, I talk. I ran out of gas on a mountain highway and a state patrolman stopped me. I realized I had left my purse with my brand new driver's license on Freda's table. The officers retreated to discuss what to do with me. I had no money to buy gas, no identification and the patrolmen had trouble with my Norwegian accent. I witnessed to the two men for forty-five minutes. Finally, they bought me some gas and sent me home.

A younger lady in her seventies lives next door. When she comes home from the grocery store, I hear her garage door opening and hurry downstairs to unload her car and carry the grocery sacks in to her kitchen. This she cannot do for herself. I mother all the elderly people around here and also care for my younger sister, who lives in Denver and is ill. These people keep me well.

The happy times nourish our spirits. Ingrid married her Kendall in August, 1984 with a celebration none of us will forget. For the ceremony and reception she chose Ski Tip Lodge, a rustic inn tucked below the Continental Divide mountains on the tumbling Snake River. On a sunny morning she crossed a flower-dotted meadow in her beautiful white dress to stand under a wildflower arch with Kendall. Afterward, musicians started up the polka, waltz, folk music and the rock young people like. All the young men wanted to dance with Ingrid's *Mormor*. When the afternoon showers came, we moved inside and danced till nightfall. Ingrid's wedding brought a smile back to my heart. And it proved I can have fun even when half of me is missing. How I yearned for Erling to see the wildflowers, to tap his fingers to the music, to share Ingrid's wedding day.

My feet still had music in them and itched for the upcoming Scandinavian Ball in autumn. I bought a new dress, a beautiful floaty blue, just made for dancing. When Erling and I went to the ball together, I had to say no to dance invitations from other men-- old Norwegian etiquette. But this evening I danced all the waltzes and many more, a wonderful party. Of course I exhausted myself. Next day I vowed to settle down, when I turn eighty-five.

Winter has come and I must spend more time at home. My apartment walls are covered with photographs, too many photographs, momentoes from a crowded lifetime. Every available surface, chests, tables, desks and lampstands accumulate pictures, stop-action scenes snatched from the flow of life. I look around and memories swarm in. A little girl pushes her sled, a *sparkstutting*. She is bundled up against the cold. Her little coat has a round collar and hangs in thick folds because it is cut so full at the hem. Trees wear a white glaze and the sun hangs low in a gray sky. A halo of gold light circles the cold, cloud-wrapped sun.

An old-fashioned group gathers on Uncle's farm... Uncle Konrad, wool-bearded, cane in hand, poses with the family in front of the salt-box farmhouse. I am the little girl in faded, flowered cotton frock. My braids are white-blond and my stockings black wool above sturdy black shoes. I look out on the world with a steady gaze. I remember how our backs ached from bending over the black earth, the spring-moist field, planting potatoes. The patient horse waited, hitched to a little farm wagon piled high with potato starts. The meadow beyond shone green against the snow-spotted mountains. The trees had put forth little light-green leaves.

161

A budding girl has her Confirmation picture taken in homemade dress and white shoes. Tomorrow shines in her eyes.

Another picture shows Oslo, its narrow streets spliced by street cars and flower boxes spilling blooms into the bright sunshine. The city overflows with vitality, amazing to a village girl. Then a passport photo displays a girl with bobbed blond hair, sweetness and yearning in her eyes. Part of a stamp for England shows on the torn-out page. The date is 1919.

A broad tree-lined avenue in Paris frames a confident woman walking with broad steps. She wears a nurse's uniform. The black wimple on her head makes her look like a nun. But a show of leg in sheer flapper-era stockings dispels this image. A baby girl is on her right arm and smiling Phillipo, curly haired and bright-faced, strides beside her on short legs, stretching his arm up to hold her left hand.

Here is something precious to me: A mother-daughter portrait. I smile from the photograph wearing pearls and a waved Mary Pickford hairdo, beside round-eyed, round-faced baby Freda. I have dressed her in a dainty embroidered smock and brown hair wisps above her frightened-fawn brown eyes.

I hunt in one of my picture books for a photo of my beloved Crown Prince Olav on his first ski outing in 1907. His stately father, tall and lean with black moustache, holds the prince's mittened hand. His tiny mother, Maude, skis in hat and motoring veil. This same Olav reigns as King of Norway today.

On my lampstand sits a black and white candid. Erling and me. We pose for the nervous cousins on our wedding day in 1939. I run my mind over the brief, precious months before the Nazis shattered our lives.

A sculptured bust of my brother, Kristoffer, dominates a color snapshot from Steinkjer. He became famous, the literary champion of the Norwegian working man. His likeness, displayed in a Steinkjer park, is mounted on a stone column which bears his life dates, 1878-1961. A street in town is named after him. Poor Kristoffer, my grown up brother, so blessed and so cursed. Bergliot, his artist-wife, died at forty, too young. Kristoffer's daughter, the one I cared for, contracted bone cancer as a child. Surgeons removed a big piece of bone from her leg. She suffered terribly, then died at thirteen. Her ordeal almost killed Kristoffer. His son, a portrait artist, died in his prime, at 40 like his mother. I look at the picture for a long time. Kristoffer is so like *Farfar*. Their faces merge in my mind, two spirits changing places in one image.

Ah! Freda and the girls making music together. Freda is smiling

My oldest sister, Anna, gazes at Steinkjer's stone bust of Kristoffer, Norway's poet of the workingman.

up from the piano, encouraging twelve-year old Ingrid, who is playing the oboe. Little Katie concentrates on her flute, a beginner who must work to keep up. Teen-aged Karin, long wavy hair flowing past her shoulders, is looking at her music, preparing to sing. She sang so beautifully. Family happiness flows out of that picture. I linger with it.

Erling, leaning over a riotous flower bed in Washington Park, is tending roses. A profusion of petunias vies for attention behind him and a blaze of something yellow stretches beyond. His muscled arms and big hands are deft among the roses.

Next comes my favorite, the color ski photograph. I take the framed enlargement down from my wall. A *National Geographic* photographer snapped the picture when the magazine covered Keystone's cross country race the winter before Astrid's death. We were all together. All five girls, plus Freda, Sam, Erling and I are smiling amid a jumble of bright red-yellow-blue ski wear. Astrid looks elegant leaning against her skis. Elisa has thrown an arm around young-teen Ingrid. Karin is calm and happy beside me. Sam, tan and silver-haired, stands above Freda. Katie, in braids and a wide, frank eleven-year old grin, straddles her mother's knee. Erling stands a head taller than anyone, in a brown and beige Norwegian knit ski sweater, corduroy knickers and brown patterned stockings. The winter sky is blue behind him. I scan the faces over and over again. Light shines from these faces. Life, energy, enthusiasm burst from this family picture like the dazzle from facets of a diamond.

My pictures are my jewels, some mellow like old rubies, some flaming like sapphires.

I look over my life while I wait. She waits for death, you might think. No! I am waiting for the New World, the new earth that the Bible promises. I believe it is coming quickly. My loved ones and I will rejoice together to enter this new creation.

Isaiah, prophet of the Old Testament, wrote: *They that wait upon Jehovah shall renew their strength. They shall rise up on wings as eagles. They shall run and not be weary. They shall walk and not faint.*

With renewed strength, I wait. I watch. I hope.

Our greatest joy: Ingrid's wedding. On a golden summer day we smile. (L.-r.) Katie, Freda, Ragna, Kendall, Ingrid, Sam, Elisa.

She's Still
　　Going Strong Today. . .

　　Ragna Dahl, age 86 at this writing, still maintains an active pace that would leave some younger persons behind and breathless. She boosts her vigorous good health with an exercise program that includes walking or cross-country skiing every other morning. On alternate days, Ragna goes door-to-door witnessing for the Kingdom. She still jokes and talks with everyone--mailmen, meter-readers, shopkeepers, policemen--and surprises some with an impulsive bear hug. She attends her Kingdom Hall meetings three times weekly.

　　She traveled alone to Norway for a three months reunion with relatives and friends in the summer of 1986 and was thrilled to experience Midsummer's Night in her home town of Steinkjer. Before her departure, she approved final details of this book's manuscript, title and cover design. Although she has kept house for herself in a comfortable apartment in Wheat Ridge, a Denver suburb, Ragna planned a late 1986 move to Dillon. She will relocate to the beautiful high mountains of Colorado's Summit County where her daughter Freda lives. She will be a frequent visitor to Summit County's ski areas and cross-country trails.

　　Whether Ragna Dahl is skiing or plying her guests with homemade Norwegian cookies and her own fragrant coffee, she retains at 86 an irresistible charm. Her young, fresh spirit, her contagious sense of humor, her joy combine with old-country ways and a Norwegian-laced English to make a refreshing personality. She is, in a word, herself!

You Can Order *SEASONS IN THE SUN* at the
Special Introductory Price Now!

For a special gift or just to share with a friend, order
extra copies of *Seasons in the Sun* at the pre-publication
price of $9.95. Ragna Dahl's warm, witty real-life story has
delighted numberless readers with its nostalgic view of
early-1900s Norway, its agonizing tale of Nazi occupation
in World War II Oslo, its high jinks, adventures and
tragedies. Both young adults and mature readers will
treasure this wholesome, human and inspiring personal
story.

Clip out coupon below and mail to:
   Seasons in the Sun, Box 1888, Dillon Colorado 80435.

Please mail *Seasons in the Sun* to me:

   Name_____

   Address _____

   City _____ State _____ Zip _____

SEASONS IN THE SUN $9.95

   Tax (Colorado only)   .49

Check or money order only. Make payable to:
   Seasons in the Sun.

Total Enclosed $_____

Send to: Seasons in the Sun
                    Box 1888
                    Dillon, Colorado 80435

Please autograph my copy: _____
                          (Name of Recipient)